General editor: Graham Ha

CW00570880

Brodie's Notes on W

# The Woman in White

Graham and Barbara Handley

First published 1980 by Pan Books Ltd

This revised edition published 1993 by
THE MACMILLAN PRESS LTD
Houndmills, Basingstoke, Hampshire RG21 2XS
and London
Companies and representatives
throughout the world

ISBN 0–333–58067–2

Typeset by Footnote Graphics, Warminster, Wiltshire
Printed in Great Britain by
Cox & Wyman Ltd, Reading

# Contents

# Preface

The intention throughout this study aid is to stimulate and guide, to encourage your involvement in the book, and to develop informed responses and a sure understanding of the main details.

Brodie's Notes provide a clear outline of the play or novel's plot, followed by act, scene, or chapter summaries and/or commentaries. These are designed to emphasize the most important literary and factual details. Poems, stories or non-fiction texts combine brief summary with critical commentary on individual aspects or common features of the genre being examined. Textual notes define what is difficult or obscure and emphasize literary qualities. Revision questions are set at appropriate points to test your ability to appreciate the prescribed book and to write accurately and relevantly about it.

In addition, each of these Notes includes a critical appreciation of the author's art. This covers such major elements as characterization, style, structure, setting and themes. Poems are examined technically – rhyme, rhythm, for instance. In fact, any important aspect of the prescribed work will be evaluated. The aim is to send you back to the text you are studying.

Each study aid concludes with a series of general questions which require a detailed knowledge of the book: some of these questions may invite comparison with other books, some will be suitable for coursework exercises, and some could be adapted to work you are doing on another book or books. Each study aid has been adapted to meet the needs of the current examination requirements. They provide a basic, individual and imaginative response to the work being studied, and it is hoped that they will stimulate you to acquire disciplined reading habits and critical fluency.

Graham Handley 1990

A close reading of the set book is the student's primary task. These Notes will help to increase your understanding and appreciation of the novel, and to stimulate *your own* thinking about it: *they are in no way intended as a substitute* for a thorough knowledge of the book.

Page references in these Notes are to the Penguin edition of *The Woman in White*, but as each chapter is separately analysed, the Notes may be used with any edition of the book

*Preamble* in the Penguin edition is often called I in other editions. Students should therefore make allowance for this if they are using a different edition, since the chapters in the first section will be differently numbered.

# The author and his work

Wilkie Collins was born in 1824 in London, the son of William Collins, a painter; he was named after Sir David Wilkie, who was one of his father's sponsors and an eminent painter and Royal Academician in his own right. Wilkie was privately educated and later travelled abroad with his parents in Italy. Some time after this he decided to become a writer, though his father had destined him for a business career. Collins published a biography of his father after the latter's death.

He became friendly with Charles Dickens and was attracted to the somewhat unconventional life of the writer, who was on the look-out for experience. Collins published his first novel, *Antonina*, in 1850; the setting was Rome in ancient times. Collins was launched on the career he had chosen, and with reasonable success. *Basil* was published two years later in 1852, and the following novel *Hide and Seek* was written in the genre of suspense and sensation that he was to make his own.

Collins's friendship with Dickens bore the double fruit of keeping him in close contact with one of the best editors of the day, who could be relied upon to further his career and to stimulate his abiding interest in playwriting and acting (Dickens was to appear in Collins's play *The Frozen Deep*). Dickens was also the editor of an influential magazine with a wide circulation, *Household Words*. He had contributed both his own novel *Hard Times* (1854) Mrs Gaskell's fine novel *North and South* (1855) to that journal. Collins thus had an outlet for his novels and shorter works of fiction, and when *Household Words* gave way to *All the Year Round*, still under the editorship of Dickens, Collins continued his contributions. Dickens obviously regarded him as an asset in terms of his particular talents — collections of his stories had been successful — and claims have been made that Wilkie was among the closest of Dickens's friends over a number of years. Collins had, in fact, a great test with *The Woman in White* (1860), in following *A Tale of Two Cities* (1859) in *All the Year Round*. But Dickens was too experienced an editor to have mistaken his man; he referred in his advertisement to the fact that he hoped in the pages of his magazine to print 'some sustained works of imagination that may become a part of English Literature'. He succeeded at once, for Collins's work was an immediate popular hit — it was subsequently, of course, to become a literary one — and its impact boosted the magazine sales above those it had enjoyed during the publication of *A Tale of Two Cities*.

Thackeray and Gladstone were among the champions of *The Woman in White*; strangely, many of the reviews were against it, largely on account of the narrative techniques employed. The book was even noticed by *The Times*, though not favourably. Collins now obtained a source of income when some of his earlier novels and stories were republished. The success of *The Woman in White* guaranteed its successor *No Name* which also appeared in *All the Year Round*. The 'sensation novel' had arrived, and the financial rewards were good: £4,600 for *No Name*, and £5,000 for *Armadale*. But his great success of the later sixties was unquestionably *The Moonstone* (1867), also issued as a serial by Dickens. Collins's novels were widely read, and *The Moonstone* cemented his reputation; it has been greatly praised by T. S. Eliot, one of the most influential writers and critics of the twentieth century.

Ironically, with the death of Dickens, Collins himself seems to have gone into a literary and physical decline. His later novels include *Man and Wife* and *Poor Miss Finch* but he was never again to scale the heights of *The Woman in White* and

*The Moonstone*. Undaunted, he went to America for a series of public readings in 1873–4 (again following in the footsteps of Dickens), and these were certainly successful. His health, however, always uncertain, began to give way as he had increasing recourse to drugs to alleviate pain. Laudanum was at once his solace and ultimately his ruin.

During the last fifteen or so years of his life Collins published a number of novels and stories, but these reflect a loss of his original power – though in many cases there was the compensation of high sales. He died in 1889. He had lived with Caroline Graves, arranged her marriage, and then had her return to him after the death of her husband. But he also had a strong attachment to Martha Rudd, who bore him three children that were suitably recognized in his will.

By Victorian standards, then, Collins was an unconventional man and was regarded with a certain suspicion, but he had sired a brand of fiction that was to have many descendants in the twentieth century. His major works constitute a fine achievement. He raised the 'sensation' novel to literary excellence, conferring on that subgenre a respectability perhaps equivalent to that conferred by Scott on Jane Austen in his celebrated review of *Emma*. Even as late as George Eliot's time the novel was still regarded, in terms of serious art, as somewhat inferior to poetry and the drama. It would be wrong to place Collins in the ranks of the great writers, but his best work shows a fresh approach, the ability to experiment in narrative art, the capacity to generate atmosphere and maintain tension – to create, in fact, an illusion of mystery and interest that keeps the reader in a state of anxiety to learn the truth. If his plots are complex (and certainly that of *The Woman in White* is), he at least offers an intellectual framework of discovery for the participating reader. And if we remember some of the fine writers who were influenced by

Collins, who absorbed, in the phrase of Henry James, the lesson of the master, we recognize the debt owed to him by writers of the standing of Dorothy Sayers and Raymond Chandler. Collins's legacy, despite the passing of time, is still our excitement.

# Plot summary

The incident recounted by Millais to his son as to the possible origin of 'the woman in white' is described on p.11 of the Introduction in the Penguin English Library edition of the novel. Here, however, we are concerned with the plot itself. It is known that Collins had read an account of a sensational Paris lawsuit, in a book which he had purchased in Paris in 1856. The case concerned a Madame de Douhault who was kidnapped; she tried in vain to get in touch with her friends, but she was imprisoned under the name of Blainville and those to whom her letters were addressed never received them. After an interval her death was presumed and, as a result, her evil brother obtained part of her coveted estate. Eventually a friend managed to obtain her release, and the prisoner's white was restored to her when she was freed. Although her friends knew her identity, she never succeeded in regaining her property from her brother. As Kenneth Robinson puts it, 'The drugging, the incarceration in an asylum, the obliteration of identity, even the detail of the white dress, all point to this once-famous French case as having provided the basic threads from which Wilkie wove the gloriously intricate plot of *The Woman in White*.'

As Robinson further notes, Collins decided that the crime of substituting one person for another and establishing that Lady Glyde was dead, was too 'ingenious' for an Englishman; hence Count Fosco was conceived. The title came to Collins when he was looking at the North Foreland lighthouse, when he is said to have thought, 'You are ugly and stiff and awkward; you know you are as stiff and weird as my white woman . . . White Woman . . . Woman in White . . . the title, by Jove!'

It is in the narrative of Mrs Catherick that the subterranean plot of *The Woman in White* is found. Sir Percival Glyde's parents were not married, and in order to establish his claim to the title and the property, he persuades the young Mrs Catherick to get him the keys to the vestry so that he can make a false entry in the register concerning his parents' marriage, thus legitimizing his own claim. This occurs in the year 1827 (the action of the novel is largely 1849–50); Mrs Catherick receives presents from Sir Percival, but of course she learns his secret and loses her respectability in the eyes of her husband and neighbours, who suspect her of having an affair with Sir Percival. In fact her child is another's (Philip Fairlie's), so that she and Sir Percival come to an arrangement whereby each keeps the other's secret; Sir Percival decrees that she must reside in Welmingham, where she lives down her past and achieves respectability. She disobeys him, however, and takes her daughter Anne to Limmeridge, where the child is befriended by Mrs Fairlie, wife of the man whose affair with Mrs Catherick resulted in Anne (hence the strong resemblance to Laura, who is really her half-sister).

Sir Percival arrives at Limmeridge, abuses Mrs Catherick and shouts at Anne, whom he calls an idiot; Anne warns him that she will reveal his secret if he is not careful. Thereupon her mother and Sir Percival, intent on preserving their own secrets, have Anne incarcerated in a private asylum. Aided and abetted by the faithful Mrs Clements, Anne succeeds in escaping from the asylum – hence her encounter with Walter.

Now the main plot within the narrative begins. Sir Percival Glyde, heavily in debt, is intent on marrying Laura for her money. Count Fosco has saved his life and consequently Sir Percival is in *his* debt. Their long-term aim would appear to be the possession of Limmeridge House too. Madame Fosco is a Fairlie, though virtually disinherited – so there is also a motive of revenge.

The Count, the prime mover in the action, discovers a marked resemblance between Anne Catherick and Laura and realizes that a question of mistaken identity can provide the answer to their needs. Anne must be substituted for Laura, and Laura must be imprisoned in the asylum in place of Anne. Accordingly Fosco makes every effort to learn of the whereabouts of Anne, and suceeds. Anne dies of heart disease and her death is passed off as that of Lady Glyde. ←

*[margin note: hence Walter's meeting with Anne over the grave. They will never meet again.]*

Laura, setting off after her half-sister Marian, comes to London. She is still in a weakened state, and Fosco explains this to two medical men who see her. In effect she is sedated, and the dead Anne Catherick's clothes are put on her. Sir Percival has written to the asylum to expect her, and Laura is removed there as Anne Catherick.

It is strong-minded Marian's determination to get to the truth that finally achieves Laura's freedom; Walter's return from abroad ensures that the culprits are pursued and trapped. Sir Percival dies in a church fire, and Fosco is killed by the Brotherhood. The Count's narrative (from p.618 onwards) is really a summary of his part in the plot, and details the complexity and timing of it. With Sir Percival dead, Walter and Laura marry and their child becomes the 'Heir of Limmeridge'. Presumably they live happily ever after: 'let Marian end our Story'. But, sadly, this splendid woman does not have a story of her own.

# Chapter summaries, critical commentary, textual notes and revision questions

## Preamble

This is a simple statement, which indicates the method to be adopted in the novel, i.e. that the writer of these introductory remarks will occupy the role of the narrator but will then give way to other narrators, each of whom plays a part in the story and will see it and relate it from a different perspective.

Note at once the directness of the style. The law analogy is deliberately stressed – each narrative is in effect a testimony, with the reader acting as judge and jury. The final statement is almost like the call to enter the witness box.

**the lubricating influences of oil of gold** i.e. the influence of money.

**and his task** i.e. his responsibility in fully telling the tale.

## The First Epoch, the story begun by Walter Hartright
## Chapter 1

This is used to (a) establish the atmosphere on the evening in question and (b) to bring out the function of Pesca in the plot. There is also a series of glances back into the past. Pesca illustrates Collins's sense of the unusual, even grotesque, here though in sympathetic ambience. The element of chance is stressed in Pesca's accident, and again this is an important strand in the structure.

**Hampstead** This fashionable north London suburb would at this time have been an attractive village.

**that he had left Italy for political reasons** This is the period of the struggle for Italian unity. The great leader Mazzini came to England and gained much support here.

**impromptu**  i.e. on the spur of the moment.
**the steps of the machine**  i.e. of the bathing machine.


## Chapter 2

Walter Hartright goes to see his mother and sister at Hampstead; at his mother's cottage he meets Professor Pesca and then tells the story of his friendship with the little Italian, and how he (Hartright) had saved his life at Brighton.

Pesca has his particular function in the story, for he has discovered that a Frederick Fairlie, of Limmeridge House, Cumberland, 'wanted to engage the services of a thoroughly competent drawing-master, for a period of four months certain' (p.43). He elaborates on the duties, and urges Walter to apply for the post. Walter is hesitant but sends his testimonials; Mr Fairlie accepts his services.

Notice the eccentricities of Pesca, and Collins's penchant for detail – facts are essential in this story of multiple deception. The scene of family interaction is done with verve.

*energy*

*Collins was probably
fond of his family.*

**precipitate**  Quick, speedy.
**Set**  i.e. of crockery.
**apostrophising**  i.e. exaggeratedly praising.
**a naked head**  i.e. bald.
**Dante**  Dante Alighieri (1265–1321) the great poet of Italy, a remarkable influence on Western literature. He is best known for the *Divine Comedy*.
**Hell of Dante**  In the first part of the *Divine Comedy*, 'Inferno', Hell is divided into successive circles – Pesca would naturally be familiar with the details.
**deuce**  Plague, mischief, the devil take it.
**a recommend**  i.e. a recommendation.
**My seat was on thorns**  Pesca, being foreign, has only half-absorbed English clichés and proverbs.
**We don't want genius in this country**  ... Collins has a gift for satirical observation, and this is a good example.
**phlegm**  Coolness, sluggishness.

**four guineas a week** In those days, a large sum of money.
**unexceptionable** Perfect, to which no one could 'take
 exception'.
**starting** Should be 'stating', an obvious misprint here.
**caprice** Whim, impetuous reaction.
**our national grog** A whimsical way of referring to alcohol.
**When your sun shines in Cumberland** Pesca's own
 idiosyncratic adaptation of the proverb 'Make hay while the sun
 shines.'


# Chapter 3

Walter takes leave of his mother and sister, and makes his way
home across Hampstead Heath, where he has his strange
encounter with 'the figure of a solitary Woman, dressed from
head to foot in white garments'. He listens to her appeal and
they walk towards London, she speaking mysteriously of a
Baronet who has done her an injury. She also speaks of
Limmeridge Village; this is, of course, the place in Cumberland for which Walter is bound. They reach London and
Walter gets her a cab. On the way back he sees two men in a
chaise and they ask a policeman if he has seen the woman in
white who, they say, has escaped from an asylum.

 The rise in narrative tension is immediate – the atmosphere
lulling and almost soporific beforehand. Notice the detail of
the description, and the dramatic and sharp nature of the
dialogue. The effect of coincidence – again a strand in the
structure – is immediately present with the mention of Limmeridge. The whole chapter shows Collins's ability to make
and maintain dramatic tension.

Cousing sleep

**Finchley Road ... Regent's Park** The interested student can
 trace Walter's route on any good street map of London and its
 suburbs.
**St John's Wood** Now a fashionable suburb of north-west
 London; then, like Hampstead, little more than a village.

**a fly** A hired carriage pulled by a single horse.

**to humour her in such a trifle** i.e. to give in to her because of such a small thing.

**affrightedly** i.e. fearfully.

**trunpike ... turnpike man** The gate set across the road to stop carts and other vehicles passing until their drivers had paid a levy or toll. The turnpike man collected this.

**Tottenham Court Road** Important shopping thoroughfare leading from Oxford Street to Hampstead Road.

**an open chaise** i.e. a carriage, which could be of any size.

**Asylum** Private asylums were fairly common at the time; the checks on what constituted mental illness were not as rigorous as they are today.

## Chapter 4

Walter is conscience-striken when he realizes that he might be responsible for the escape of a potentially dangerous patient, yet is inclined to believe in the truthfulness of the woman he has helped. He travels north, but his arrival at Limmeridge House is delayed by the railway. As soon as he arrives he goes to bed, attended by a 'solemn servant'.

The balance is struck between the pressures of Walter's conscience and the journey north: Collins is merely moving the narrative forward, but it is still tense with expectation.

**Carlisle ... Lancaster** We do not intend to gloss English place-names outside London, but the interested student will obviously check the actual details of Walter's journey.

**discomposed** Agitated, ruffled.

**out of livery** i.e. not in his correct uniform.

## Chapter 5

Walter wakes, and looks out on a fine view. When he goes down to the breakfast-room, he meets Marian Halcombe, who introduces herself as one of his pupils and explains the situation within the house. She proves an interesting companion, explaining that her mother was twice married, so that Laura Fairlie is her half-sister. Walter describes her 'gracefully bantering way'; Marian is witty if not pretty, and provides Walter with a good deal of information about his future life-style. Walter is moved to tell her of his adventure with the woman in white, and how that lady mentioned Mrs Fairlie. Then he receives a message that he is to see Mr Fairlie.

The introduction to Marian carries the due weight of the unexpected – a favourite Collins' device which we might call the 'conning' of the reader. We are struck at once with her frankness and her natural fluency. Walter is intent on making the connection between Mrs Fairlie and the woman in white.

**The easy elegance ... The lady is ugly** One of Collins's unexpected twists.
**maxim** A general truth, principle, rule.
**restorative** i.e. calculated to restore her strength.
**crabbed** Cross-grained, perverse, irritable.
**unaccountable** Which cannot be explained rationally.
**cardinal virtues** i.e. best points (of character).
**backgammon** Game played on double board with draughts and dice.
**écarté** Card-game played by two people.
**fidget one** i.e. make one uneasy.

## Chapter 6

Walter's charming sitting-room in Mr Fairlie's house is described. The servant then shows him into Mr Fairlie's room and announces him to that idiosyncratic, eccentric hypochondriac. Mr Fairlie's obsession with his coins and examples of art is indicated, together with his great obsession with the state of his nerves. Walter examines Mr Fairlie's collection of 'really fine specimens of English water-colour art', and survives the interview and Mr Fairlie's languid self-indulgence really suggests that he is not in-phase with the real world.

and simulated suffering. When he leaves the large, lofty, magnificently furnished room Walter feels that it is 'like coming to the surface of the water after deep diving' (p.71).

Here Collins shows himself to be adept at creating another kind of atmosphere – that of a stifling and claustrophobic nature. Mr Fairlie is another grotesque. Note again the detailed description of the room, Collins being intent on giving us the atmosphere of place. The affectations of Fairlie are finely consistent – he is a parasite. Collins is satirising the quality of his egoism and the nature of his withdrawal from life.

**Raphael's name** i.e. the great Itailian painter (1483–1520).
**chiffoniers** Low cupboards with sideboard tops.
**buhl and marquetterie** Kinds of furniture inlaid with patterns.
**Dresden china** Of the kind produced in Saxony, especially in the eighteenth century.
**tempered** i.e. held at bay.
**listlessly composed** A fine phrase to describe Mr Fairlie's physical apathy.
**frock-coat** A man's long-skirted coat not cut away in front.
**a wash-leather stump** i.e. for cleaning the coins.
**to possess you** Note the affectation of this: he means 'to have you with us'.
**quite cast my insular skin** i.e. I have ceased to be English in my tastes (the analogy is with a snake shedding its skin).
**Goths in Art** i.e. barbaric, having no taste.
**Charles the Fifth** (1500–58) Significant ruler – of Spain and Emperor of Germany.
**Titian** The great Italian painter who ranks with Michelangelo and Raphael at the forefront of the Italian Renaissance (1477–1576).
**pecuniary arrangements** i.e. the salary you are to be paid.
**tablettes** i.e. sheets from his note-pad – another affectation.
**Rembrandt** The celebrated Dutch portrait (and historical) painter (1606–69).
*Can* **you undertake them** i.e. get them into good condition.
**plebeian** i.e. common.

**straining** i.e. clearing.

**It was like coming to the surface of the water** A rare Collins image, but notice the connection with Walter's saving of Pesca's life.


## Chapter 7

Walter meets Mrs Vesey, Mrs Fairlie's former governess, then, in the summer house, Laura Fairlie. Walter describes in some detail his own portrait of her. Apart from his glowing description, Laura herself is charming and considerate, and Walter has obviously fallen in love with her at first sight. When she says 'I shall believe all that you say to me' he is won, and realizes that he is in danger of forgetting his own position; he becomes aware, too, of the contrast between Marian and Laura. They spend a delightful evening in the drawing-room, with Laura playing Mozart; later Laura and Walter go on to the terrace. Then Marian reads aloud part of a letter that could shed some light on Walter's meeting with the mysterious woman in white; there is an account of Mrs Catherick's child, Anne, who also, apparently, dressed in white. The last sentences of the letter indicate her resemblance to Laura Fairlie – 'a white figure alone in the moonlight', as Walter sees her.

Laura passes to and fro without hearing while the letter is being read, and does not seem to know what they have been discussing.

The integration of Walter into the household is accomplished. Although this is a long chapter, most of its importance is included in the summary above, with the role played by Marian increasingly important as she provides, from the letter she is reading, the essential links with Anne Catherick *and* the connection with Laura. The latter's movements as Marian reads add to the tension: the end of the chapter, with

shows her innocence.

Walter seeing Laura as the woman in white, is a brilliant forecasting of what is to happen later in the plot — the one woman substituted for the other.

**Mrs Vesey *sat* through life** A fine piece of casual Collins irony.

**Nature was absorbed in making cabbages** i.e. people who think little and do less.

**brightened dimly ... went out again** Note the image, almost Dickensian in the suddenness of its caricature.

**parasol** Sunshade.

**Sympathies that lie too deep ... for thoughts** An echo, perhaps unconscious, of Wordsworth's 'Thoughts that do often lie too deep for tears.' (*Ode on Intimations of Immortality.*)

**Let the kind ... Let her voice ... Let her footstep** Typical rhetorical Collins flourish, achieved through repetition, one of his common devices.

**wanting** i.e. lacking.

**pet feathers of vanity all unruffled** Marian can turn a neat phrase, and here she goes one better and turns a neat image.

**that generous trust in others** A pointer to Laura's character, and hence to her suffering with Sir Percival Glyde.

**The grandest mountain prospect ... appointed to annihiliation** The smallest human interest that the pure heart can feel is appointed to immortality. Perhaps one of the more sententious of Walter's utterances, and one doubts that it will stand up to close analysis.

**white muslin. It was spotlessly pure** An unobrusive symbolic indication of Laura's innocence and simplicity — and of her connection with Anne.

**half ... in soft light, half in mysterious shadow** Again symbolic of the deepening mystery to come.

**Mozart** Wolfgang Amadeus Mozart (1756–91), the famous musician born in Salzburg, composer of *The Magic Flute* and *Don Giovanni*.

**ottoman** A sofa with neither back nor arms, often used for the storage of clothes or blankets.

## Chapter 8

Laura, tentatively questioned by Marian, has but vague recollections of Anne Catherick. Walter now knows that he is in love, and the days and weeks pass and confirm in him his deep feelings for Laura. But she changes towards him, obviously putting herself on guard; Marian is about to enlighten Walter.

This contrasts with the previous chapter, since it marks the passage of time, long enough for Walter to fall in love, long enough for Laura to do so too, but to conceal it by a change of behaviour. Romance again deepens to mystery.

**the track of the golden autumn** Note that the style is consonant with Walter's romantic mood.

**Our words are giants ... injury** An example of Walter's occasional eloquence.

**enervate** To deprive of energy.

**raillery** i.e. wit and banter.

**as coolly as I left my umbrella** A homely image, but a memorable one.

**talisman** A charm, something capable of working wonders.

**like a smooth stream with a swimmer ... current** A suitable image when one remembers Walter's saving of Pesca.

**Syren-song ... fatal rocks** In Greek mythology, temptresses who, with enchanting music and song, lure unwary sailors to shipwreck on the rocks on which the syrens sat.

## Chapter 9

Near the end of the third month of Walter's stay, he and Marian are left together after breakfast. Marian intercepts a letter for Laura, but then allows the gardener's boy to take it on into the house. Then she tells Walter that he has been foolish in allowing himself to become attached to Laura, but Marian's manner is kind and sympathetic. She adds that Walter must leave Limmeridge House – not because of his position but because Laura herself is engaged to be married.

Marian also reveals that Laura, in turn, cares deeply for Walter, and that he must therefore leave for her sake as well as his own. Again there is mention of Walter's adventure with the woman in white, and then Laura's maid comes to tell Marian that Laura wishes to see her. Walter learns that Laura is engaged to Sir Percival Glyde, a Baronet, who lives in Hampshire – hence again the association with Anne Catherick.

This shows Marian's warm and sympathetic nature, both in her caring for Laura and indeed her care for Walter once she has told him of Laura's coming marriage. But this sadness soon gives way to mystery. The interception of the letter, Marian's subsequent remarks, the whole turn of Walter's mind, sets him putting two and two together.

**prescient** i.e. forecasting.
**'I canna tak' it on mysel'** i.e. I cannot let myself be responsible for . . .
**avowal** Sworn statement.
**like a bullet to my heart** Note the simple effectiveness of the statement.
**Knight, or Baronet** The Knight's ('Sir') title is not hereditary, but the Baronet's is.

## Chapter 10

As he sits in his studio setting Mr Fairlie's drawings in order, Walter's mind is crowded with unhappy thoughts of Laura and her fiancé Sir Percival Glyde. He knows that he has no reason to wonder, as he does, whether there is a connection between Sir Percival and the woman in white, who was ill-treated by a Baronet from Hampshire. Laura's likeness to Anne Catherick also plays its part in directing Walter's suspicion to Sir Percival, and Hampshire is Anne Catherick's native place.

There is a knock at the studio door and Marian Halcombe enters; she has brought with her an anonymous letter addressed to Laura (which was delivered to the gardener's boy by an elderly woman). Marian hands the letter to Walter to read. It tells of the writer's prophetic dream of Laura's wedding day and warns Laura that only great distress can come to her if she marries the man in the dream. There follows an accurate description of Sir Percival Glyde, though the writer does not mention his name. The last sentence of the letter, 'Your mother's daughter has a tender place in my heart – for your mother was my first, my best, my only friend', again directs Walter's suspicions to a connection between Sir Percival and the woman in white.

Walter and Marian discuss the letter, which they agree must have been written by a woman – and one whose mind is probably deranged. They set off for the village to see if anyone there can shed light on the identity of the elderly woman who delivered the letter.

This is powerfully dramatic – the dream is ominous – and adds to the tension over the coming visit of Sir Percival Glyde. Again notice the detail with which Collins is at once describing and laying clues for the alert reader – and for the doubly alert Walter now that he fears losing Laura.

**jog-trot acquaintances** Casual and dull.
**Genesis xl.8, xli. 25; Daniel iv. 18–25** The first deals with Joseph's interpretation of Pharaoh's dreams, as does the second, while the third is Daniel's interpretation of Nebuchadnezzar's dream about the tree.
**a monomania** An obsession.
**He has fought ... contested elections** Note the irony implicit in the author's tone.

## Chapter 11

Enquiries at the village school indicate that one of the lads, Jacob Postlethwaite, has seen 'T' ghaist of Mistress Fairlie'.

This was in the churchyard, and the woman was dressed in white; Walter is convinced that the 'ghost' and the writer of the letter are one and the same – Anne Catherick. He visits Mrs Fairlie's grave, where he finds that the gravestone has recently been partially cleaned. Walter then goes to see an old woman whose husband is responsible for looking after the grave. She tells him that her husband has been ill for some time, but hopes soon to be able to clean the gravestone. Walter goes back to Limmeridge House, and notices Laura Fairlie walking on the gravel below; he then returns to the churchyard and keeps watch of Mrs Fairlie's grave.

A chapter replete with mystery and some Gothic overtones, with the child's story of the ghost. Again Marian plays a leading part in the action, here through her interrogation, but the most moving part of the chapter consists of Walter's watching Laura. Note the emphasis on place, the creation of a lonely and isolated atmosphere which is consonant with Walter's mood at the prospect of having to part from Laura.

**forlorn little Crusoe ... solitary penal disgrace** A fine and pathetic image. The novel *Robinson Crusoe*, written by Daniel Defoe (1661–1731), was published in 1719.
**t' ghaist** i.e. the ghost.
**Yestere'en, at the gloaming** i.e. yesterday evening, at twilight.
**yander, in t'kirkyard** i.e. over there, in the churchyard.
**your story at your fingers' ends** i.e. you know exactly what you are planning to say.
**a trifle** i.e. a small amount of money.

## Chapter 12

Soon Walter hears footsteps approaching, and the voice of a woman reassuring her companion that she has safely delivered 'the letter'. Presently Walter sees two women, one wearing a blue cloak covering a dress of white. The older woman walks on, and Walter wonders whether he should follow her, but he stands near the grave in order to see the younger woman. He finds that she is indeed Anne Catherick. Walter tells her of the two men he saw who said that she had escaped from an asylum. Anne reveals that Mrs Fairlie was a great friend, that Mrs Clements is her present helper, and that she (Anne) did not get on well with her own mother. Walter taxes her by telling her that she has made Miss Fairlie unhappy by sending the letter. Another reference to the fact that Anne had been put into an asylum arouses her passion; she says she is frightened of losing herself. When Sir Percival's name is mentioned she screams incessantly, and it needs the arrival of Mrs Clements to allay her fears. Before she goes, Anne kisses the marble cross on Mrs Fairlie's grave.

The churchyard scene is full of suspense, with the dramatic effect achieved by Walter's listening to the two women. But the recognition of Anne Catherick and the ensuing convincing dialogue is exactly right and very moving. Walter's compassionate nature is seen at the end of the chapter when Mrs Clements takes care of Anne.

**warrant** i.e. guarantee.
**profaning marks** i.e. signs of desecration and suffering.
**artless** i.e. innocent.
**sentient** i.e. having the power of sense perception.
**a private asylum** Run by a proprietor who might or might not be qualified.
**to say me nay** i.e. to contradict me.
**who had placed her under restraint** i.e. had her put into an asylum.
**I shall lose myself if you talk of that** i.e. I shall lose my reason, my mind.

## Chapter 13

Walter tells Marian all his news; she in return says that Sir Percival will have to convince her and the solicitor Mr

Gilmore that he was not responsible for confining Anne Catherick in an asylum unjustly. The next day is Walter's last day – he has Mr Fairlie's permission to leave, or rather the latter 'waives his right of refusal', which is typical of his indolence. Meanwhile Marian reveals that Anne Catherick has left with Mrs Clements; she has seen the news of Laura's forthcoming marriage to Sir Percival Glyde. Marian tells Walter that Sir Percival will have to explain everything if he is to marry Laura.

There is little to add to the summary above. Marian again shows her impulsive warmth by taking Walter's arm when she realizes that Mr Fairlie – with no effort on his own part – has released him from his contract. Tension is of course provided by the news that Anne and Mrs Clements have gone.

**note-paper as smooth as ivory ... thick as cardboard**  Note the contrast, typical of Mr Fairlie's pseudo-artistic preferences.
**waives**  Forgoes, relinquishes a right or claim.
**I had ... man's insolent letter ... the woman's atoning kindness**  Note the fine antithetical balance of this construction.

## Chapter 14

Mr Gilmore arrives, and Walter indulges his own morbid introspection in view of the fact that this is his last night at Limmeridge House. Then he meets Mr Gilmore, who announces that he will be contacting Glyde's solicitor, and that he has arranged for the two women (Mrs Clements and Anne Catherick) to be traced. Mr Glimore feels that Sir Percival is a completely upright and sincere man; Walter believes that he is quite the reverse. The evening is spent in high tension, with Laura playing the piano as a kind of background to the various emotions – but she does say that she will get up to say good-bye to Walter in the morning. When, next morning, Walter sees her for the last time he discovers

– as he already half-knows – that she loves him too. But she cannot break her engagement to Sir Percival. Thus ends Walter's narrative.

This is a fitting climactic sequence to Walter's narrative. Gilmore is given the customary detailed treatment, and Walter is given the usual natural background which is consonant with his mood. The evening is charged with sentiment and emotion, the morning with the cold light of day irradiated by the warmth, the tremulous warmth, of Laura's love. The whole chapter shows Collins as superbly the writer of mood.

**sanguine** Hopeful, confident that things will go well.
**The leaves fell about me** Note that the decay in nature
  corresponds to Walter's mood.
**draggled** Wet, limp and trailing.
**disputation,** i.e. argument.
**Good shooting ... preserved** i.e. kept and preserved for game
  (pheasant, etc.) with the owner having the shooting rights.
**Bon voyage** i.e. good journey.
**I would fain have** i.e. I would have wished to.

## The story continued by Vincent Gilmore Chapter 1

This immediately links with Walter's narrative, since the account is written at his request; it is a factual report of Mr Gilmore's stay at Limmeridge House.

First, he notes the decline in Laura Fairlie's appearance, then the unchanging negation of Mr Fairlie's attitude and manner. When Sir Percival Glyde arrives he refers to the anonymous letter of his own accord, and urges Marian to write to Mrs Catherick, asking her to confirm why her daughter was committed to an asylum. Marian complies, and after the letter is written Glyde asks some searching questions about any possible encounters Anne may have had with occupants of Limmeridge House; he also enquires where she was staying. He then goes to his own room.

Left alone, Marian and Mr Gilmore talk for a while. She accepts that they have no reason to doubt Sir Percival's explanation but communicates some of her misgivings to Mr Gilmore.

This reflects Collins's facility in adapting the style to the nature of the narrator. Note the exactitude of the report, almost legalistic in tone, and thus contrasting with Walter's own subjectivity in the previous chapters. Yet even here Gilmore shows his susceptibility to Marian, who in so many ways is the real heroine of the story.

**a life-interest** i.e. only during his own lifetime does he own the property.

**adverting** i.e. referring to.

**great beauty of the Law ... can dispute** Collins is here ironic at the expense of legal procedure.

**Water-Colour Societies** i.e. of practising water-colour artists.

## Chapter 2

Sir Percival is in a very good mood at dinner, and two days later the confirmatory letter about Anne's being 'placed under medical superintendence' arrives from Mrs Jane Anne Catherick. Marian discusses Sir Percival with Mr Gilmore; she says she cannot accept the responsibility of persuading Laura to marry him; Mr Gilmore puts the legal standpoint. He learns later that Laura is begging for time before coming to a decision.

Mr Gilmore goes to see Laura, and explains to her the object of the marriage-settlement. Laura is intent upon having Marian to live with her after the marriage, and is determined to leave some money to her half-sister. She also hints that she would like to leave Walter something.

Sir Percival invites Mr Gilmore to visit him at any time; Mr Gilmore, impressed, returns to London.

While this is geared to confirmation of Anne's state and Sir Percival's integrity, the tone of the narrative is all against us accepting what appears to be factual. Collins is exposing the reality beneath what appears, and consequently the reader is keyed up for some revelation which will expose Sir Percival. Once Marian becomes suspicious, we are with her despite the evidence. Gilmore, as I have said, is susceptible, nowhere more so than in his being reminded of the happy Laura he knew as distinct from the bowed down Laura he knows now.

**caprice** Whim, the mood of the moment.

## Chapter 3

This opens with a letter from Marian to Gilmore announcing that Laura's marriage to Sir Percival will take place before the end of the year. Gilmore then explains the legal implications of the marriage, which are strongly beneficial to Sir Percival both in his own lifetime and, should she die first, after Laura's death. There is also the question of the disinheritance of Philip Fairlie's sister following her marriage, some time ago, to Count Fosco.

On Gilmore's advice, Marian also would benefit from Laura's will but Sir Percival's lawyer objects on the grounds that the entire £20,000 should go to Sir Percival if his wife died first. Gilmore appeals to Fairlie about it; the latter character-istically, refuses to intervene.

Gilmore now meets one of the 'sharp practitioners' – Mr Merriman, Sir Percival's solicitor. He reveals that Sir Percival is trying to trace the old woman and Anne Catherick, and is keeping a man in London [Walter Hartright] under surveil-lance. Later Gilmore sees Hartright in London; Walter, dis-tracted, says he is going abroad.

The revelations begin – the atmosphere changes almost

completely in this sequence. The overall effect is one of unease because of the emphasis on the financial situation of Sir Percival. The contrast between the two legal men is well brought out. Notice the cunning plot control which removes Walter completely from the area of action, so that we are left to speculate what will become of him as well.

**abstract** i.e. summary.

**stipulation** A condition insisted upon.

**In default of issue** If there were no children.

**at a dead-lock** i.e. unable to resolve things.

**sharp practitioners** i.e. clever people with an eye on the main chance.

**inveterate good humour** Always happy, never appearing to be put out by events.

**he won't take it off** i.e. he has made me responsible for a particular course of action.

**the fag end of a tune** i.e. the last strains or notes.

**Euston Square ... Holborn** The interested student should consult a map of London, particularly a 19th-century one if possible, which will indicate the City and those areas not yet 'built up' – though they too would be thickly populated.

## Chapter 4

Gilmore returns to Limmeridge. He has an unsatisfactory interview with Mr Fairlie, who refuses to object to the settlement Gilmore now finds so repugnant from Laura's standpoint. At the end of his narrative, Mr Gilmore says, 'No daughter of mine should have been married to any man alive under such a settlement as I was compelled to make for Laura Fairlie.'

An ominous chapter, since Gilmore comes out strongly against the present settlement. Mr Fairlie grows even more repugnant – the human characters, even later in the novel, Fosco – are so much more acceptable than this arid imitation of a man.

**palpitations** Throbbings, increased activity of the heart owing to exertion, agitation or disease.

**usual room ... usual chair ... usual aggravating state** Note how the repetitions convey the monotony and dull state of Mr Fairlie's existence.

**smelling-bottle** i.e. containing smelling-salts or a similar restorative.

**Radical** i.e. desiring reforms, belonging to the extreme of the party (perhaps here meaning Liberal).

**maundering** Talking listlessly or in a dreamy manner.

## The story continued by Marian Halcombe Chapter 1

Marian describes an interview with Laura, who is proposing to tell Sir Percival that she loves another man hoping that this will oblige him to release her from her engagement. Laura's manner with Sir Percival then becomes more relaxed; she arranges to speak to him the next day. Marian receives a letter from Walter, saying that he has been watched in London. Then Laura, who doesn't know of this, speaks to Sir Percival of her love for another, but he says that he will not withdraw from the engagement, and indeed affects to love her the more for her confession. As Marian says of Laura, 'Her own noble conduct had been the hidden enemy, throughout.' Laura tells Sir Percival that she can never love him, but he refuses to break off their engagement. Laura resigning herself to what she feels is her unavoidable marriage, requests Marian – if she, Laura, should die first – to write to Walter and tell him that she had loved him.

Marian does write on Walter's behalf to see if she can find him a situation. Sir Percival sees Mr Fairlie, who feels that all is now settled. Marian is very upset at the thought of the marriage going ahead; she takes Laura away for a holiday, and learns that Walter has sailed for South America.

The stress in this chapter is on the strong sympathetic nature of Marian's narrative, and the unnaturalness of Sir

Percival's reaction, which could – but doesn't – reflect his own sympathetic understanding of Laura. The latter is impassioned and brave. Notice how effective the diary form of narration is – Collins is once more distinguishing his narrators by marks of their own individuality. The album of Walter's drawings is the symbol of Laura's love – it also shows her immaturity, the childlike way she clings to her love. At the same time, it is movingly pathetic.

**first last outburst of tenderness** Note the fine economy of the phrase.

**paroxysm** i.e. a fit.

**impressibility** i.e. being affected strongly (by an idea or emotion)

**Honduras** A maritime republic of Central America.

## Chapter 2

The marriage is fixed for 22 December. Laura is upset that it is to be so soon, and there is an emotional scene between herself and Marian. Laura makes Marian promise that she will not tell Walter about the event, and Marian in turn decides to conceal from Laura the fact of Walter's departure for Central America. Sir Percival later proposes a wedding tour that will take in Florence, Rome and Naples; Marian describes the gradual, inevitable preparations for the wedding. Sir Percival questions Marian about Walter Hartright; she learns that Sir Percival and Laura are to meet Count Fosco and his wife in Italy. Marian see-saws emotionally in her attitude towards Sir Percival, and the day before the wedding she satirically describes Mr Fairlie's reactions towards 'Dear Laura'. Marian watches over her beloved half-sister the night before the wedding, and then, 'They are gone! I am blind with crying – I can write no more –'

(The First Epoch of the story closes here.)

Another sequence full of foreboding (Marian's word). Marian's function is effectively to protect and sustain, Walter at a distance as well as Laura immediately. Her moods reflect the inevitability. Every now and then her impetuosity breaks out. The brevity of the final entries shows Marian choked with emotion, the style reflecting her state.

**fasten our helpless lives ... a dog to his kennel** Note the appropriateness of the image, which echoes the imprisonment of Anne Catherick.

**depository** i.e. recipient.

**etiquette** Manners, behaviour, code of conduct.

**the inexhaustible mine** A deliberate hyperbole.

**Trinta del Monte assisted Sir Percival's escape** Note the parallel with Walter's saving Pesca.

**levity** i.e. light-heartedness.

**pretty little white bed** Note the tone, which somehow makes Laura childlike and innocent, and consequently emphasizes the pathos of her situation.

## Revision questions on the First Epoch

**1** Write a character study of Marian Halcombe as she appears (a) in Walter's narrative and (b) in her own diary entries.

**2** Which do you find the most dramatic incident in this epoch, and why?

**3** Give some account of Collins's style in these sections: you might consider his use of dialogue and description for a start, and refer to anything else which you find distinctive.

**4** Compare and contrast Mr Gilmore and Sir Percival Glyde.

**5** What use does Collins make of coincidence in this first epoch?

**6** By a careful attention to the text, show how Collins creates a particular atmosphere in any three or four scenes in this section.

## The Second Epoch, the story continued by Marian Halcombe Chapter 1

Marian is established at Blackwater Park, awaiting the return of Laura and her husband from their honeymoon tour. She describes the place, and speculates on the whereabouts of Walter in Central America. She also ponders on the disappearance of Anne Catherick. Gilmore, meanwhile, is ill, and has gone to Germany to rest. Fairlie is obviously relieved to be rid of the women of the house.

Laura's letters to Marian have not been exactly revealing, since she has said nothing about her husband's character and conduct. Marian finds a wounded dog, apparently shot by Baxter, the keeper; she learns that it is Mrs Catherick's dog. Mrs Catherick had called the previous day, but had left when she found Sir Percival was not at home. Meanwhile, the dog dies.

Marian's contemplation of Blackwater Park shows Collins once more building an atmosphere, in some ways a carefully contrasting one with that of Limmeridge. The transition also marks the passage of time, with the major event, the marriage, occurring off-stage, and thus heightening its drama by us not knowing exactly what has happened. It is typical of Marian's comprehensive sympathy that she should think of Walter, but we are aware of her own sense of isolation. But the incident with the dog is the prefiguring symbol — wounded and in pain until it dies, the animal anticipates the treatment meted out later to Anne Catherick. Marian's compassion is again called out by this experience. Collins's detail of description is remarkable.

**Tyrol** District in North Italy and Austria traversed by three
ranges of the Alps.
**on a dead flat** i.e. a uniformly even piece of land.
**famous highwayman's ride to York** Marian is referring to Dick
Turpin.

**condemned to patience, propriety, and petticoats** A good example of Marian's wit – alliterative and self-ironic at the same time.

**journal** A form of diary – a fashionable occupation for young women who were not over-employed was to write it up in some detail each day.

**in producing sun-pictures** See note p.648 Penguin English Library Edition. Photographs taken by natural light.

**Tiglath Pileser** The name of three Assyrian kings, the most notable being Tiglath-Pileser I (*c*.1115–*c*.1093 BC) and III, known also as 'Pulu', who reigned 745–727 BC.

***The Smudge*** Note the irony of this – Collins is mocking how ridiculous certain collectors' items are.

**social martyrdom** i.e. cut off from ordinary social life.

**It is always Laura Fairlie ... never Lady Glyde** Note how aptly Marian sums up, and prepares herself for the duality of Laura's life.

**antiquity** i.e. his ancient home.

**George the Second** (1683–1760); King of Great Britain.

**basement** The ground floor is meant here, as will be obvious in later chapters. The word 'basement' was first used in this sense in 1730, and was probably so used occasionally in Collins's time.

**frouzy** (A variant of 'frowzy' or 'frousty'); ill-smelling, fusty, musty.

**allegorical leaden monster** i.e. representing some mythological figure.

## Chapter 2

This chapter marks the return of the couple from their honeymoon. Marian finds Laura much changed; she will not discuss her married life. She asks about Walter, but Marian says that she has neither written to him nor heard from him lately. Marian notices Sir Percival's 'mania for order and regularity'; he often appears annoyed.

Count Fosco and his wife have accompanied Sir Percival and Laura to Blackwater Park, and Marian describes them – Countess Fosco first; Marian mentions her changed appearance and her jealousy and possessiveness over the Count. Fosco makes a strong impression on Marian from the first moment of their meeting: 'He looks like a man who could tame anything.' She then goes into detail about his fatness; his likeness to Napoleon; his manner; his fondness of his 'cockatoo, two canary-birds, and a whole family of white mice'; his knowledge and conversation; 'his tact and cleverness'. She also notices his attitude towards Sir Percival. The day after the party's arrival Merriman arrives to see the Baronet.

The highlight is the introduction into the action of Count Fosco, a major force in the structure of the plot. As with Pesca and Mr Fairlie, we are aware of a grotesque element. Laura is impetuously warm – that is her nature – and this makes her concealment over the nature of her marriage all the more effective. The force of Fosco's personality is immediately evident, seen markedly in the reactions of his wife, whom he has tamed apart from her inherent jealousy of her disposition. He is power personified, but there is more to it than that. The mystery at the end of the chapter establishes a high note of tension.

**mania** i.e. obsession.
**love-locks** i.e. curls of hair.
**cold as a statue ... impenetrable as the stone** Note the continuance of the image, which carries its own definition of the kind of person the Countess is.
**Henry the Eighth** (1491–1547); King of England, who severed the Church of England from the rule of the Pope in Rome. He had six wives.
**Alexander the Sixth** Obtained the position of Pope, by bribery, in 1492; he fathered children, among them the celebrated Lucrezia and Cesare Borgia.
**Napoleon** The great French emperor and general, finally defeated by Wellington and Blücher at Waterloo (1815).
**pagoda** The mouse-cage is shaped like a pagoda – a sacred building of pyramidal form in India, China, Burma etc.
**organ-boy** i.e. the player of a street organ.

**petrifying** Converting into stone (or a substance as hard as stone).
**Chi sa?** Who knows?

## Chapter 3

Laura is to be asked by Sir Percival's solicitor Merriman to
sign a document; obviously Sir Percival is in debt and needs
some money. Marian plays chess with the Count. The following day Sir Percival wishes to see everyone in the library, but
instead the entire party go off to view the lake. Sir Percival
and the Count discuss the lake; later the Count holds forth on
a variety of topics. He loses one of his mice, but recovers it.
Blood is discovered under the bench of the boat-house by the
lake; Marian tells the story of the wounded dog and speaks of
the visit of Mrs Catherick. Sir Percival is obviously discon-
certed, and leaves to question the house-keeper about Mrs
Catherick's visit. As soon as he has gone, Count Fosco avidly
plies Marian with a host of questions about this visit. Later,
back at the house, Sir Percival recovers his composure and
says that he wants the Count and Countess to witness 'a
signature – nothing more.'

Notice that Marian overhears the conversation between Sir
Percival and Merriman, a favourite device for conveying information – or part-information. The paradox in Fosco's
character is seen in his love of his pets (or is it a kind of
sadistic possession?), but he also displays his cynicism about
crime and the nature of criminals.

**bills due at three months** i.e. which had to be settled three
months after the money was paid on loan.
**dog-cart** Two-wheeled driving cart with two back-to-back seats
across its width.
**heavy claims** i.e. financial demands
**Nankeen** Kind of yellow cotton cloth (originally from Nanking in
China).
**Barber of Seville ... Figaro** The first, the famous opera by

Gioacchino Rossini (1792–1868); the second, its leading character.

**St Cecilia** The Roman Saint and martyr, patron saint of music.

**Figaro qua! Figora la!** In this aria the busy little barber of Seville is complaining that he is at the beck and call of everybody.

**the Dead Sea** A sea or lake in Palestine, the waters of which evaporate since it has no outlet. They are intensely salty.

**Rights of Women** *The Vindication of the Rights of Women* was written by Mary Wollstonecraft in 1792; this is being ironically echoed here.

**clap-trap** Uninformed nonsense.

**I am a citizen of the world** A deliberate literary echo of *The Citizen of the World* by Oliver Goldsmith (1728–74), and the ensuing remarks re John Chinaman and John Englishman are related to it.

**bonbon** The French word for a sweet.

**Chocolate à la Vanille** A type of vanilla-flavoured chocolate confectionery.

**John Bull** He epitomizes the supposedly typical Englishman.

**John-Howard-Philanthropist** He was indeed a noted philanthropist, celebrated for his prison reforms (1727–90).

**Chatterton** The celebrated English poet who committed suicide at the age of 18 (1752–70).

**Sheridan** The celebrated dramatist (1751–1816), who wrote *The Rivals* and *The School for Scandal*.

**Benjamin** Youngest child, darling.

**mellifluous** Sweet toned, sweet sounding.

**Isaac of York ... Brown Molly** Isaac of York was the name of Rebecca's father in *Ivanhoe* by Sir Walter Scott (1771–1832). Brown Molly was probably just a common name for a horse.


## Chapter 4

Both Laura and Marian refuse to sign, despite the uncompromising attitude of Sir Percival. Fosco remonstrates with Sir Percival, who leaves in the dog-cart. Marian meanwhile writes to Gilmore's partner and puts the letter in the post-bag in the front hall: Count and Countess Fosco are standing just outside the front door of the house. The Countess asks Marian to accompany her for a walk in the grounds – the Count immediately returns indoors. The Countess keeps Marian walking for some time; she finally gets away from the Countess, and as she enters the house she sees Fosco in the act of dropping a letter into the post-bag – from which, of course, he may have previously removed it.

This centres around the letter after the refusals to sign, which obviously raise the dramatic temperature. The influence Fosco exerts on Sir Percival is a further demonstration of his power. Marian is sensitive to Laura's feelings for Walter. The revelation in this chapter is the cunning of the Countess, obviously ordered into action by the Count. The tension is being consummately maintained – we are anxious to know exactly what is going on, but are being kept in the dark by the unflagging skill of the narrator.

**cast in my teeth** The equivalent of 'thrown in my face'.
**a splitter of straws** i.e. one who dwells overmuch on trivial details and explanations.
**crochets** Possibly a misprint for 'crotchets': whims, peculiar habits.
**sullen submission of a tamed animal** Fine image to indicate the dominance and power of the Count.
**you made a virtue of necessity** 'To make a virtue of necessity' is a direct quotation from Shakespeare's *Two Gentlemen of Verona* Act IV, Scene 1.
**apologist** i.e. defender.
**unencumbered** i.e. not weighed down by.
**the post-bag** This would be used by the occupants of a large Victorian country house for letters awaiting collection.


## Chapter 5

In the evening Marian and Laura go for a walk in the grounds, and Laura confesses the unhappiness of her marriage. She has innocently mentioned Hartright to Sir Percival, who senses that she loves Walter and tells her that she will bitterly repent it. Later when she and Marian are by the lake they see a figure, almost certainly that of a woman. When they return to the house the Count and Countess are there. Obviously they have not been out.

The mystery deepens in this chapter. We feel for the sufferings of Laura, and also for those of Marian on her account. Laura's confession about her feelings for Walter shows her living martyrdom at having to be Lady Glyde. Mystery surrounds the figure by the lake – is it a man or a woman? – but this maintains the narrative tension.

**Women can resist a man's fame ... how to talk to them** A good example of Collins's casual wisdom and his ability to put it succinctly.

**as a fish in a pond outside** An apt simile for the Countess.


## Chapter 6

Marian is contemplating in the night whether to slip out and wait for the messenger from the solicitor in London. She does so later, and the letter advises her to urge Lady Glyde to withhold her signature until he, the solicitor, has given his advice. Immediately after receiving the letter Marian meets Fosco, who escorts her back to the house. Sir Percival greets them gloweringly from the steps. The Count has a chat with him, and reports to Marian that the Baronet has now changed his mind about the signature.

Marian has a frightening vision or dream – called by her a day-dream – in which Walter reveals that one day he will return. Shortly after this Laura appears and tells her that she has just seen Anne Catherick, who has found Laura's missing brooch. Anne has told Laura that she loves the name of Fairlie, hates that of Glyde, and says that she has been waiting for days to speak to Laura. She blames herself for the marriage, stresses her past fear of Sir Percival, but says that now she is dying. She has however, 'The Secret', with which she can still threaten Glyde. After that she leaves. Laura can remember no more, despite the promptings of Marian. Later, the Count and Sir Percival return from their walk; their respective moods are changed. A chill in the air presages a change in the weather next day.

Much is resolved, or at least explained, in this chapter. Actions at night always produce excitement, and there is certainly that here. Kyrle's letter is unequivocal in its advice. The Count's attitude may cause some surprise, but we are always aware of his cleverness, and suspect that he is really organizing what may best be done – for himself and Sir Percival. Laura's news of her meeting with Anne Catherick means that this chapter never flags in terms of action and interaction. In some ways her description alerts us to the deception which is going to be practised later on – the stress of resemblance between Laura and Anne is typical of Collins's clue-laying. The chapter ends on an ominous note – the Count's prophesying a change in the weather symbolizes a change in tactics too.

**Made a party to** i.e. that she enters into the conspiracy.
**as if he had sprung up out of the earth** Rather like the Witches in *Macbeth*.
**lowering** i.e. darkening with temper and frustration.
**felicitations** Good wishes and greetings.
**immense ruined temple ... tropical trees** Note the grotesqueness of the dream, which in some ways is akin to the menacing atmosphere of Blackwater Park.
**exhalations** Breathing-out; here possibly of a poisonous smoke.
**to hail the hindmost boat** i.e. shout to the last one.
**Pestilence ... Arrow ... Sea** Note how the personifications help to make the dream larger than life.

**his watch-chain ... like a golden serpent** Note the evil inherent in the image.

**like a spring ... my heart** One of Collins's triter images.

## Chapter 7

On 19 June it is raining heavily, and the morning is passed indoors. Laura goes out after lunch; she is followed to the plantation by Marian who, unable to find her, goes back to the house. On arrival Marian discovers that Laura, already returned, has been locked into her bedroom, and the door guarded by a stupid, lumpish housemaid. Laura's own personal maid Fanny has been summarily dismissed by Sir Percival. Marian is forbidden to enter Laura's room: she taxes Sir Percival with this, and the Countess, strangely, supports her; the Count overrules Sir Percival.

Marian sees Laura, who has found a note from Anne telling her that she was followed by Fosco. Sir Percival had seen Laura retrieving Anne's note from the sand by the boathouse, gripped her strongly, and forced her to give him the letter. Marian says that she will write to Mr Gilmore's partner and to Mr Fairlie, for Sir Percival has threatened to get out of Marian and Laura everything he thinks they know.

Again a chapter full of action and incident. Anne's letter is particularly moving, Marian's courage in this adversity as strong as ever. But the movement by which Laura is imprisoned is ominous, and we feel that the attitudes of the Count and the Countess are built on duplicity.

**ante-chamber** A room leading to a main apartment.

## Chapter 8

Marian feels that someone may have entered her room while she has been talking to Laura; then she meets Madame Fosco and the Count. The latter flatters Marian, much to his wife's annoyance. Marian writes urgent letters for help to the lawyer and to Mr Fairlie, then returns to Laura's room. She goes to the village with the letters, and gives them to Fanny: the one to the lawyer to be posted in London; Mr Fairlie's to be delivered by hand when Fanny reaches Limmeridge.

On her return to Blackwater Park Marian learns that Laura has again been threatened by Sir Percival. He is to have a talk with the Count, who pointedly asks Marian if she has any letters for the post. Then Fosco detains Marian while he talks and plays music. Eventually Marian retires to her room and writes up her journal.

The atmosphere of apprehension dominates this chapter, with the feeling that everything Marian does is watched. We marvel at Marian's stamina and her resilience to the situation. The friction between Sir Percival and the Count indicates the baronet's anxiety about his financial circumstances and further conveys the need for action.

**Neapolitan** i.e. from Naples.
**La mia Carolina** i.e. my Caroline.
**Oratorios** Semi-dramatic musical compositions usually on sacred themes.
**Symphonies** Elaborate musical compositions for full orchestra.
**Rossini** See note p.39. *Moses in Egypt* and *Guillaume Tell* are two of his compositions.
**recititavo** i.e. musical declaration.
*sotto voce* In an undertone, aside.

## Chapter 9

Marian leans out of her window; she smells the tobacco smoke of the two men talking below. She changes her clothes, and decides to venture out on to the flat roof outside her bedroom. She becomes cold and wet, but is able to eavesdrop on the men's conversation outside the library window below. She learns that her letters have been discovered, and that the Count is much the cleverer of the two men. Sir Percival is virtually without any money at all. Fosco puts up the idea that if Lady Glyde were to die, Sir Percival would be £20,000 better off, and Madame Fosco would also get her legacy of £10,000. Percival asserts that he must find Anne Catherick, and tells Fosco of Walter's thwarting of him at every turn. Fosco says he will find Anne, and then learns, to his astonishment, that she is very like Lady Glyde. We are left, as Marian is, with the idea that there is a new idea in the Count's mind.

Once more the effective use of the eavesdropping technique. Marian's later illness is prepared for by her enduring the cold and the damp, but really this chapter serves to reveal the main elements, though not the complexities, of the plot, and we understand now why Fosco is involved, for there is the certainty that his wife would benefit if Laura dies – and we know what that means. Collins builds up an atmosphere of tension by detailed description before Marian overhears the two men talking. There is little doubt that Sir Percival's outbursts against Walter derive from jealousy. The cunning and deeper duplicity of the Count is well conveyed.

**Eau sucrée** i.e. sugared water
**I walk ... upon egg-shells** Perhaps Fosco has not quite got his command of idiom here – perhaps he means that he is treading uncertainly.
**maudlin** Mawkishly sentimental.
**Paid down** i.e. at once, in cash.
**scribble-scrabble** i.e. scrawl hurriedly and carelessly.
**scrapes** i.e. troubles.
**as sweet on** i.e. in love with, caring for.
**exhibition of Punch** i.e. Italy, where the puppet shows originally started.

## Chapter 10

Marian is in a fever after her exposure to the cold and the drenching rain during the night on the roof; she is obviously going to be ill. There follows a NOTE by the author, then 'POSTSCRIPT BY A SINCERE FRIEND', as Fosco takes over, and the diary expresses his sentiments for Marian, who is now ill.

This is a remarkable narrative turn, demonstrative again of Fosco's power and ingenuity. There is little doubt that he is much taken with Marian.

**stratagem** i.e. manoeuvre, cleverness, cunning.

## The story continued by Frederick Fairlie, Esq., of Limmeridge House

Mr Fairlie, as we can imagine, is annoyed at having to write the narrative. Fanny has called to see him with a letter from Marian. She tells of a visit she had from the Countess, how she drank some tea and fainted; when she came to she found that she still had the two letters, but that they were crumpled. Fanny further reveals that she is frightened of Sir Percival. When she has gone, Mr Fairlie reads Marian's letter and feels threatened by it. He will not open Limmeridge House 'as an asylum' (note the word) to Lady Glyde. He has also heard from Gilmore's partner that the latter has received an envelope in Marian's handwriting, with a blank sheet of paper inside. Next he has a visit from the Count, who says that Marian is too unwell to leave Blackwater Park; in fact she still has a severe fever. He has also come to tell of the disagreement between Sir Percival and Lady Glyde. He asks Mr Fairlie to receive Lady Glyde. Mr Fairlie, anxious to get rid of Fosco, writes an extremely short and casual letter to Laura – so that he will at last have peace of mind!

This section of the narrative – note the use of contrast with the previous section and with the animation of Marian's style – enables Collins to indulge his irony at the expense of the narrator. It is a study in self-pity and selfishness. All Fairlie is concerned with is what he calls being 'upset for the day'. The interview with Fosco strikes a comic note. At the same time, Fairlie reveals (despite the effort) a striking turn of phrase. He also reveals a certain pride in being single and a distinct prejudice against the superiority married couples sometimes evince. Fairlie obviously has no moral scruples, his sole wish is to be left to himself in indolence, cocooned from the vulgarity of experience.

**Goths and Vandals** The Goths, a Germanic tribe that invaded and devastated Europe in the third to fifth centuries. The Vandals, another fierce Teutonic tribe, destroyed the works of art and literature in Rome (AD 455).

**in the lower orders** i.e. the lower (servant) classes.

**propriety** Good manners, proper behaviour.

**struck of a heap** i.e. frightened, flabbergasted, amazed.

**ostentation** Showing off.

**solemnized** Here (ironically), celebrated.

**prosy** Dull.

**recipient** The receiver of

**labyrinth** A maze.

**temporising** Indecisive, time-serving.

**epistolary** In the style of a letter.

**lacerating** Mangling, tearing.

**walking-West-Indian-epidemic ... typhus by the ton** Note the colour and effect of the description – and how perfectly it conveys Mr Fairlie's fears and prejudices.

**fumigating** Disinfecting with fumes.

**siesta** i.e. afternoon rest or sleep.

## The story continued by Eliza Michelson Chapter 1

The housekeeper at Blackwater Park writes of Marian's illness, and Laura's intense worry about her sister. Marian had refused a mixture put up by Fosco, and a doctor called Dawson had been sent for. Marian continues to decline, and Laura sits up with her. Meanwhile, Fosco sends away for a nurse to relieve Mrs Michelson. The foreign nurse Mrs Rubelle arrives, and it is arranged that she will enter on her duties the next day. The doctor objects to Mrs Rubelle, and speaks to Mrs Michelson about this, she can find nothing wrong with Mrs Rubelle's treatment of her patient. The Count and Sir Percival now begin to query Dr Dawson's treatment. The Count goes away for a week; Marian appears to improve, and faith in Mr Dawson revives. Marian deteriorates again; the Count returns, and a London physician is sent for.

The Count and Mr Dawson disagree over the nature of Marian's illness, but the physician pronounces that it is indeed typhus fever as Fosco had said. Laura, who had entered the room earlier, is led out in a state of collapse. Five days pass, with Laura constantly visiting Marian; by the 10th day Marian is much better. Laura, however, collapses. Dawson leaves after a dispute with the Count, and there is thus no medical attendance for Laura or Marian. Then Sir Percival says that all of them will be leaving, and orders Mrs Michelson to dismiss the servants, with the exception of the stupid housemaid Margaret Porcher.

This narrative is outside the main stream, since the housekeeper is not a major character. This again shows Collins's skill in contrast – this narrative is factual reportage – but the power of evil and the cunning displayed by the Count are both evident between the narrative lines. The introduction of Mrs Rubelle is ominous, and we feel the trap closing around Marian in the first instance and Laura in the second. Even more ominous is the closing up of the house and the sacking of the servants.

**saline** Impregnated with salt or salts.
**heresy** Opinion contrary to orthodox opinion.

**blind errors of Popery** Mrs Michelson is obviously prejudiced against Catholics, as she might well be, being the widow of a Church of England clergyman.

**Creole** i.e. here she means 'of mixed blood', European and Negro.

**a quack** i.e. a fake.

**with a handle to his name** i.e. possessing a title.

**mesmerism** The practice of the hypnotic state usually rendering insensibility to pain, produced on the patient by the operator's force of will.

**reprobated** i.e. expressed disapproval of.

**typhus fever** A highly infectious disease, marked by the eruption of purple spots, high temperature, prostration and delirium.

**in lieu of** In place of, instead.

## Chapter 2

Mrs Michelson is herself intent upon leaving, but first she sees Sir Percival and the Count. They had pretended to plan that Marian and Laura should go to Torquay accompanied by Mrs Michelson. The latter, worried about Marian, goes to Torquay but finds that there are no lodgings available; when she returns she finds that the Count and Countess have left for St John's Wood. They have apparently taken Marian with them, and Laura is terribly upset when Sir Percival tells her. Marian, he says, is on her way to Limmeridge; Laura later tells Sir Percival that she must go after her. Sir Percival writes to Fosco, arranging for him to meet Laura on her arrival in London. Laura is very suspicious, particularly about Mr Dawson leaving, and Marian being forced to travel. Next day Laura takes leave of Sir Percival, implying that it is their final separation. She thanks Mrs Michelson for her kindness to her and to Marian.

Later Mrs Michelson meets Mrs Rubelle in the garden, and learns that she and Marian have not left Blackwater Park. Mrs Michelson wishes to resign, for she feels that her trust has been betrayed, but she is taken by Mrs Rubelle to see Marian, where she has been hidden, with Mrs Rubelle in attendance, in the disused wing of the house. Mrs Michelson decides to stay in a room nearby, with the gardener also within reach should he be needed to give assistance. Sir Percival's temper breaks out before midnight, and he drives madly away. Later Marian leaves for Limmeridge House. Mrs Michelson finishes her account, but can't remember the exact date on which Laura had left.

The movements in this chapter are exercises in deception. The focus of the plan is to separate Marian and Laura, with Mrs Michelson as a kind of dupe. She represents normality, and therefore cannot be trusted by Sir Percival or Fosco for fear of what she may discover. Notice how Mrs Michelson goes along with the arrangements for Laura to go to London, though she is of course unaware at this stage of the deception over Marian. The fact that Mrs Rubelle and Marian have not left Blackwater Park is a masterly dramatic stroke. The naïveté of Mrs Michelson is shown by her faith in the innocence of Fosco – a tribute in itself to the charm and magnetic power of the man.

**pagan** i.e. not Christian.
**memorandum** i.e. containing details, making a definite statement.
**pecuniary** i.e. financial.
**take a turn** i.e. a short walk.
**A soft answer turneth away wrath** Mrs Michelson is fond of Biblical allusions, and certainly uses – as here – the proverbial ones.

### The story continued in several narratives Chapter 1, The Narrative of Hester Pinhorn. Taken down from her own statement

She explains how she got the job in St John's Wood with the Foscos, who were joined by the sick 'Lady Glyde'. The latter has a fit or convulsions, and the doctor says that it is heart-disease. Fosco appears very concerned, but the next day 'Lady Glyde' is much better. It is temporary, for she dies, and she testifies that her master Count Fosco could not have been involved in the fright which apparently caused her death.

Despite the uneducated nature of the narrator, this is a graphically effective account. The legal nature of her story is again stressed – she is 'testifying' in a simple way, uttering what she thinks is the truth and thereby exonerating Sir Percival.

**convulsions** A kind of fit.

## Chapter 2, The Narrative of the Doctor

This is merely testimony of death.

**Aneurism** Abnormal enlargement (presumably of the heart).

## Chapter 3, The Narrative of Jane Gould

This witness laid out the body.

## Chapter 4, The Tombstone

This is the inscription of 'Lady Glyde's' birth, marriage and death.

## Chapter 5, The Narrative of Walter Hartright

Walter has been wrecked, but survived and reached London in October 1850. He went to see his mother and sister, learnt of Laura's death, and sets off to visit her grave. He does so, and, after his anguish, sees two women coming towards him. One is Laura, Lady Glyde!

This is a masterly chapter, dramatic, using the unexpected with consummate art to close the second epoch of the story. The straight retrospect is overtaken by the graveyard scene (remember the earlier one) which shows that Collins has 'conned' the reader, just as Sir Percival and Fosco hoped to 'con' everybody in believing in the death of 'Lady Glyde'.

**Oh death, thou hast thy sting! oh, grave, thou hast thy victory!** Walter's way of registering his relief and recognition.

(*The second epoch of the story closes here.*)

## Revision questions on the Second Epoch

**1** Describe Marian's reaction to Blackwater Park. How important is the incident with the dog in shaping her views?
**2** Give an account of the appearance and character of Count Fosco.
**3** Show how Collins presents Sir Percival Glyde in these chapters.
**4** Indicate the part played by (a) the Countess and (b) Mrs Michelson in this sequence.
**5** Describe the importance of 'eavesdropping' in any one chapter.
**6** What do you find humorous in any parts of this epoch, and why?

## The Third Epoch, the story continued by Walter Hartright, Chapter 1

Walter explains that he is now living with his two 'sisters' in a poor neighbourhood in London, 'Alive in poverty and in hiding' is how Walter describes the position of Laura.

The effect is to bring us up to date, with the detailed retrospect through Marian's story to follow in the next chapter.

**house-forest** Perhaps a 19th-century way of describing the 'urban jungle' of London.

## Chapter 2

Walter begins to tell Marian's story. She had received a letter at Blackwater saying that Lady Glyde had died in Count Fosco's house in London. Marian goes to her solicitor, who sees Fosco, who has himself been staying at Limmeridge House. He has given details of Laura's death, but a paragraph appears in his letter saying that Anne Catherick has been found and returned to the asylum. Laura's clothes are sent back. 'Anne' has been shut up again; Marian is overcome, but recovers sufficiently to have the Fosco house in St John's Wood watched. She can't find out anything about the Rubelles, and Sir Percival has settled in Paris. Meanwhile Marian sets out for the asylum where she believes that Anne Catherick is being kept; when she sees her, she realizes that it is Laura who has been imprisoned quite deliberately. Marian persuades a nurse to let her speak to Laura alone, and then bribes the same nurse to let Laura escape.

Now comes Laura's story – how she was met by Fosco at the railway station and taken to, supposedly, Fosco's house in St John's Wood, but in reality to the Rubelles' establishment in a non-residential part of London. She faints, and is given 'water' that tastes strange. Thereafter she has very vague recollections of what happened, but has obviously ended up in the asylum under the name of Anne Catherick. Marian now takes Laura to Limmeridge, but Fairlie refuses to recognize Laura, and says that his niece lies buried in the churchyard. It is there that the sisters accidentally meet Walter, returned from abroad.

Note the skill with which Collins links the two narratives of Marian and Laura. We admire Marian's courage and her tenacity in adversity. The plot to exchange identities – the using and abusing of Anne Catherick – is now clear. Marian plays the role of a man in terms of her taking vital action to get Laura out of the asylum. Walter brings us full circle to the graveside, even implying that God has brought the three of them together again.

**the tangled web** Woven, according to the proverb, when first we practise to deceive.
**posture** Here the meaning is 'state'.
**South Western Railway** Before the nationalization of railways after World War II, the rail system was a regional one.
**infamy** Wicked, dastardly behaviour.


## Chapter 3

Now in London, Walter experiences a great sense of peril; he gets a job, and Marian runs the house. Walter prepares himself for the coming struggle with Glyde and Fosco. Laura, in her run-down state of health, could certainly be mistaken for Anne Catherick; she picks up a little through Walters encouragement, and begins to sketch again, while Walter himself sets out to gather what information he can.

The present is fraught with peril. Marian certainly undertakes her share of work, not afraid to demean herself by it. Walter shows himself to be methodical in his investigations.

**immunity** Without punishment.


## Chapter 4

Walter goes to see the lawyer Kyrle to explain about Laura. Kyrle puts the legal position; after some discussion Walter leaves the solicitor's office. On the way home he is certain he is being followed by two men. At home he finds Marian waiting for him; she has received a letter from Fosco containing a threat against Walter. They discuss Sir Percival's 'secret', (with which Anne Catherick had threatened him) and determine to find it out.

The irony of this chapter is that Kyrle puts the legal position, so that Walter – who is determined to act anyway – has to face the fact that the burden of establishing the criminality of Sir Percival and Fosco rests on him. With his return to Marian tension rises because she has received the letter. This itself has a flamboyasnce which almost distinguishes the writer. Marian's intuition (and fear) makes her believe that the Count is the more evil of the two men.

**Chancery Lane** Area in the City associated with the law.
**a metaphysical conclusion** i.e. a mere theory.
**litigation** Taking a matter to law.
**The storm's of life ... the valley of Seclusion** Almost a parody of the Biblical 'valley of the shadow of death'; the parody is ominous too.

# Chapter 5

Walter goes to Hampshire, but can't get much information. He goes to Blackwater Park, but is watched by a man in black. He returns to London, knowing that Anne Catherick, 'the woman in white', is at the real heart of the mystery. Walter decides to search for Mrs Clements who had looked after Anne. From Marian he gets details of the Glyde family and Sir Percival's early life.

There is little to add to the summary above. The initial failures here are a clearing of the way towards significant discoveries later. Collins is in fact building tension in this way.

**chattels** Movable possessions.
**carpet-bag** A travelling bag made from carpet-like material.

## Chapter 6

Walter finds that Mrs Clements is staying in the Grays Inn
Road, and she describes her journeys with Anne, and the
stages of the latter's illness. Anne had been very anxious to see
Lady Glyde. They had met the Count, who was remarkably
struck by the resemblance between Laura and Anne; he persuaded her to take some medicine, which initially had a good
effect on her. Then, says Mrs Clements, she was lured away
by the Countess Fosco, and when she returned Anne has gone.
Mrs Clements had not succeeded in tracing her.

There is genuine discovery here, with Fosco's plot in part at
least revealed: he has used the resemblance between Anne and
Laura to bring about the death of Anne, with the world
believing it to be the death of Laura.

**exonerate** i.e. clear (someone's name).

## Chapter 7

Obviously the Foscos had abducted Anne. Mrs Clements tells
Walter the story of Anne's mother. It appears (but note that
word) that Mrs Catherick had had an affair with Sir Percival
after her marriage to Catherick, who had been physically
beaten by Sir Percival. The Baronet then left the village, but
Mrs Catherick remained. Mrs Clements believes that Sir Percival, however, had continued to support her. Perhaps, thinks
Walter, the truth is not so obvious as it seems (i.e. about the
affair between Sir Percival and Anne's mother). Strangely, in
appearance Anne was apparently not like either her mother or
her father. Walter tells Mrs Clements that Anne is dead; he
then decides to seek out Mrs Catherick for himself in order to
discover the truth.

The force of this chapter is to suggest something (an affair
between Mrs Catherick and Sir Percival) which may again be

the author 'conning' the reader. Notice that from time to time Collins sets a story within the story, as here with Mrs Clements's narrative about Catherick, Sir Percival and Mrs Catherick. All the time clues are being laid, particularly about Anne and the fact that she was not like either of her parents.

**holding herself uncommonly high** i.e. considering herself to be superior to her neighbours.

## Chapter 8

Walter returns home and finds that Laura is near breaking-point. Again he persuades her to begin sketching again, and this obviously has a therapeutic value. He decides to go to Welmingham to see Mrs Catherick, who lives at number 13 in the Square.

Walter finds Mrs Catherick a very intimidating woman; he tells her that her daughter is dead: Mrs Catherick is unmoved. She complains that she has been a much maligned and wronged woman who has now won respectability. Walter says he does not believe that Anne was the child of Mrs Catherick and Sir Percival, or that their meetings were concerned with that kind of guilt. She bids him go, but obviously Walter must try to find Sir Percival if he is to discover 'The Secret'.

Despite Mrs Clements's warning Walter must go to Welmingham. This enables Collins to indulge his satire of the small town, and the nature of respectability. But there is considerable tension – again clues are being laid – and the reader is forced to speculate on the coldness and indifference of Mrs Catherick to the news of Anne's death.

**torpor** Lack of animation, lack of activity.
**arid exile ... house carcasses** Note how cleverly the symbols of the place represent the death-in-life of Mrs Catherick.
**deserts of Arabia ... our modern gloom** A fine indictment of

the soulless nature of 19th-century building – a remark that
could, ironically, apply to our own time.

**cheffonier** i.e. chiffonier, a movable low cupboard.

**wreak it** i.e. fulfil it, carry it out.

**sufferance** i.e. under tolerance.

**sitting** i.e. her own seat in church.

**I had stirred in its lair** Note the nature of the image, which
underlines the sensational or melodramatic nature of Collins's
style at times.

## Chapter 9

Walter again feels that he is being followed. He ponders on the
contempt Mrs Catherick has expressed for Sir Percival. Next
day he goes to old Welmingham Church, and afterwards sees
the clerk. He inspects the entry in the church register, and
finds a record of the marriage of Sir Felix Glyde, Sir Percival's
father. He then sets off to see the lawyer son of the previous
vestry-clerk, as he wishes to inspect the duplicate parish register kept by the late vestry-clerk. But on the way there, Walter
is again aware of being followed.

Tension in this chapter arises from Walter's movements
and the effect of his being followed.

**undersised** Surely a misprint for 'undersized'.

**betake** Taker (oneself) to.

**clandestine** Secret.

**perverse** i.e. awkward.

**subscriptions** i.e. money so that the work can be paid for.

**loggerheads** i.e. against each other.

**posted up** i.e. kept up to date.

**stretch** i.e. distance.

## Chapter 10

Walter leaves for Knowlesbury, but he is seized by two men
who have been following him, taken before a magistrate in

Knowlesbury and charged with assault. He is remanded in custody, and this is obviously what was wanted by Sir Percival and his two thugs, since the remand lasts for three days. But Walter manages to contact Mr Dawson, the doctor who had attended Marian, and thus succeeds in getting bail. He goes to see the duplicate register, and discovers that it has no entry for the marriage of Sir Felix Glyde and Cecilia Jane Elster. What he has really discovered is that the entry in the original parish register was falsely inserted at a later date, and that Sir Percival's parents were not married; consequently Sir Percival has no real claim to the title! When Walter leaves he is again attacked; this time he escapes, gets to old Welmingham, and finds that the keys to the vestry have been stolen. Arrived at the vestry, he finds that it is on fire! Walter tries to save Sir Percival, who is inside, but the supposed Baronet dies in the flames.

A highly dramatic chapter, in which Collins displays his flair for the sudden succession of events which go most of the way to uncovering the mystery and certainly the fraud. We note how carefully the structure has been planned – only the death of Sir Percival can free Laura ultimately to marry Walter. Another positive element in this chapter is the exciting atmosphere, particularly the crowd effects and the identification (which Walter can't really make) of the body of Sir Percival.

**pinioned** i.e. clasped tight (between them).
**surety** i.e. someone who would put up the money for bail.
**recognisances** Bonds that guarantee a person's position and behaviour.
**measter** Master.
**summun** Someone.
**yander** Yonder.
**heerd un** Heard him.
**loight** Light.
**hampered the lock** i.e. stopped it from working properly.

**ingine** Fire engine.
**starveling** Small, starved looking.
**Baronight** Baronet.

## Chapter 11

The inquest. Then Walter writes to Marian to tell her his news. After the inquest, he goes to old Welmingham to see the ruins of the vestry by daylight. Then he gets a letter from Mrs Catherick.

Again we are aware of the structure. The inquest being over, and the outward mystery still existing, it is essential that another piece in the jigsaw should be fitted for the reader. Hence Walter's receiving Mrs Catherick's letter.

**abstraction** i.e. taking away.
**garret-chamber** A kind of attic, very small room.
**trivial and terrible ... together** Collins has a fine sense of poignant contrasts and changes in life.
**There is nothing serious in mortality** An echo of a famous speech by Macbeth, the third line of which is 'Tomorrow, and tomorrow and tomorrow'.
**Solomon in all his glory** Again the use of a biblical quotation for emphasis.

## The story continued by Mrs Catherick

Mrs Catherick tells how Percival Glyde in 1827 persuaded her to give him the keys of the vestry. Basically, it is the story of Sir Percival's discovery of his own illegitimacy. He had found the blank space at the bottom of the vestry page, and only had to make himself out to be born prematurely to complete the forgery. He had refused, too, to clear Mrs Catherick from the imputations made against her, but makes her a financial allowance – on certain conditions. She explains how she has never liked Anne, and how at Limmeridge Anne formed the habit of wearing white. Sir Percival had insisted on Anne's being shut up. Mrs Catherick now considers that Walter owes her an apology!

The deviousness and deception revealed. At the same time as the facts given in the summary above there is also an interesting focus on the character of Mrs Catherick herself and her own greed, and more than a hint that Walter's own attractiveness has had its part in her making this confession. She has a kind of inverted morality, and of all the grotesques in the novel is perhaps the worst. Respectability is her aim at all costs. She even has the effrontery to castigate Walter for his attitude, after all her own deceptions!

**privity** A relation between two parties that is recognized by law.
**a seven months' child** i.e. premature.
**to screen** i.e. cover up.
**trumpery** Worthless rubbishy nonsense.
**incumbrance** i.e. burden.
**vagaries** i.e. changes of mood and reactions.
**Dorcas Society** A ladies' organization, meeting to make clothes for the poor: membership of this would be the height of respectability.


## The story continued by Walter Hartright Chapter 1

Walter receives a letter from Marian, with the news that she has been obliged to move. There is some discussion with Merriman on the poor estate that Sir Percival has left. But Walter keeps the fraud secret.

The main implication here is that Fosco is very much alive and operating at his usual level of vigilance. We feel the tension rising again.

**East Indiaman** A ship plying between England and the East Indies.

## Chapter 2

When Walter gets to Fulham he finds that Marian has seen Fosco, standing in the street in front of their lodgings. He was with the owner of the lunatic asylum. Obviously the Count is arranging for Laura to be taken back, and only his consideration for Marian (ashamed though she is of it) has prevented him from acting so far. He also leaves with Marian a threat against Walter. Walter is determined to pursue Fosco. Marian tells Laura of her husband's death. Walter continues his investigations and virtually proves that Anne was the illegitimate daughter of Mrs Catherick and Laura's father Philip Fairlie – hence her striking resemblance to Laura.

Marian now fills in the parallel story. But after that Walter's own intelligence leads him to a positive discovery about the real identity of Anne Catherick. We marvel at the complexity of the plot and Collins's ingenuity. Examine the detail thoroughly in this chapter, and you will find that Collins is fitting everything together exactly – the tightness of the structure is amazingly sustained.

**card-case** For carrying visiting cards.
**mountebank** Fake, charlatan.
**crape** i.e. worn for the funeral.
**mite** i.e. a very small contribution.

## Chapter 3

The great improvement in the health and spirits of Laura. Walter confides his wishes with regard to Laura to Marian. Finally Walter and Laura are married.

The romantic and sentimental conclusion which is not a conclusion since the threat of Fosco is still there. Notice that Collins is playing with the reader: marriage normally marks the end in a plot, but Collins, perhaps as fascinated by his creature Fosco as we are, goes beyond this.

## Chapter 4

Later they return to London, Walter determined to bring the Count down, though he does not confide this to Laura. He decides to consult his friend Professor Pesca, then follows the Count to the theatre, taking Pesca with him.

The reintroduction of the amiable Pesca is one of the points of contrast. The other is that Walter has been followed in the past, and the tables are turned with Fosco being followed in the present.

**Crystal Palace Exhibition in Hyde Park** The Great Exhibition, of which The Crystal Palace was the centrepiece, was held in 1851.

## Chapter 5

At the opera Pesca is being watched by a foreign-looking man with a scar on his face; then Pesca and the Count see each other. Pesca does not recognize the Count, but the Count appears to recognize him, with terror – Fosco bolts from the theatre, closely followed by the man with the scar.

Walter questions Pesca about his own past in Italy. Pesca gives him a long account of The Brotherhood and its aims. Pesca shows him the brand burnt deeply into his flesh; it appears that the Count has probably been false to the Brotherhood.

Superb drama – for the only time in the novel we see Fosco lose his control. At the same time the nature of the Brotherhood – idealistically noble – somehow makes the action melodramatic, something which Collins has hitherto succeeded in avoiding. And the Brotherhood operates in extremes, combining the nobility I have instanced above – independence for Italy – with the terrible rigour of execution.

**Donizetti's** A celebrated Italian composer who wrote sixty operas, among them *Lucia di Lammermoor*.

**political societies** See particularly the note in the Penguin
English Library edition.
**first Charles** i.e. Charles I of Great Britain and Ireland, born
1600, beheaded 1649.

## Chapter 6

Walter is convinced that the Count has defected from the
Brotherhood, and determines to go after him quickly. He
accordingly writes to Pesca to tell him that the Count has
betrayed his affiliations. He himself sets out for St John's
Wood, leaving Marian to look after Laura. Walter enters the
Count's house, having seen, in passing, the man with the scar
also approaching Fosco's house.

Marian's courage well in evidence again. Narrative expectation is aroused by the feeling that the confrontation with the
Count is imminent.

**the Seine** The river on which Paris stands.

## Chapter 7

Walter finds himself face to face with the Count. He gives him
a note that virtually ensures the Count will know his days are
numbered with regard to the Brotherhood. Walter asks for a
signed confession of the conspiracy; in return, the Count demands free passage for himself and his wife. In other words,
Walter is prepared to accept the establishment of Laura's
identity; the Count may then have his freedom. The Count
writes his version of the conspiracy; he is then cool enough to
give himself exactly one hour's sleep. He bequeaths his birds
to the London Zoo, but keeps his white mice and their exotic
cage.

A fine chapter, the bargains being struck directly, with the
Count recovered but perhaps fatalistic. Despite Walter's com-

posure, it is the Count's reactions which compel our attention. Even the detailing of the birds to the Zoo is informed with his idiosyncratic power. His attraction for Marian means that he has to refer to her before he leaves.

**my passport regulated** Presumably there was a time limit set on this, just as there is today.

**order-book** i.e. in which he kept the names of those who hired him.

**he had snowed himself up in paper** A very English image to comment ironically on the Count's mode of composition.

**bodkin** Thick blunt needle with large eye for drawing tape.

**Napoleon the Great** Napoleon Bonaparte (1769–1821); Emperor of the French, defeated finally by Wellington and Blücher at the battle of Waterloo in 1815.

**superscription** Words written above or outside – in this case, on the envelope.

## The story continued by Isidor, Ottavio, Baldassare Fosco

(Count of the Holy Roman Empire...) The list of titles, the high-flown offices, are Collins's own form of irony at the expense of the Count, who is always flamboyant, whether his language be written or spoken.

Fosco explains his reason for coming to England, repeats details we already know, and tells how he fell in love with Marian. The rest of his story is known to us through Walter's researches and the other narratives. The Rubelles were of course instrumental in changing Lady Glyde – who arrived in London after her 'own' death – into Anne Catherick, thus getting Laura into the asylum. Fosco continues, with remarkable persuasiveness, to assert his innocence!

There is little to add to the summary given above, Collins's irony having already been noted. Fosco spells everything out. His has been the master-mind behind it all. Moreover, he has constructed his plan of action meticulously. The main elements of his attitudes and practice are well defined by himself: 'I combine in myself the opposite characteristics of a Man of Sentiment and a Man of Business.' We see particularly how he handled the discrepancy in dates. We are left in a state of admiration both for the character and for his creator.

**With a Roman austerity** i.e. disciplined, without self-indulgence.
**pecuniary** Financial.
**potentates** Eastern rulers.
**Shakespeare** The greatest of English dramatists (1564–1616).
**Hamlet** Possibly Shakespeare's greatest tragedy.
**Newton** Sir Isaac, who discovered the law of gravity (1642–1727).
**Nero** Roman Emperor during AD 54–68, known for his brutality and licentiousness.
**Alexander the Great** (336–323 BC); King of Macedonia.
**quacks** Fakes, imposters.
*En route* On the way.
**metropolis** A capital city, i.e. London.
**pathetic apostrophes** i.e. moving cries or exclamations.
**self-immolated** i.e. sacrificed herself completely.

## The story concluded by Walter Hartright Chapter 1

Walter checks on the Count's story with regard to the dates concerning Lady Glyde. He now has the evidence he needs, and sets out for Cumberland. After an interview with the foolish Mr Fairlie, Walter reads the tenants a statement establishing the fact that Laura is alive and that they have attended a false funeral. The tenants see Laura and acclaim the fact that she is alive. Walter and Laura return to London.

This is a triumph for Walter, and includes the putting down of Mr Fairlie. There is the usual deft concentration on detail. There is a marked pathos when we come to the simple inscription on the gravestone.

**Brougham**  A type of horse-drawn carriage.
**statuary's**  i.e. the man responsible for erecting and carving the gravestone.

## Chapter 2

Pesca and Walter go to Paris; the man with the scar on his cheek is seen by them; on the way to Notre Dame Cathedral Walter passes the Morgue. He returns and enters it, and sees people passing before the dead body of Fosco. The Brotherhood has exacted its revenge. The Countess lives on in Versailles, and tends her husband's grave.

This is another conclusion, this time a contrasting one. Yet the style elevates Fosco rather than degrading him – a signal mark of authorial affection for his larger than life creature.

**Victor Hugo**  The great French dramatist, novelist and poet (1802–85).

## Chapter 3

Birth of Walter's and Laura's first child; later, Marian and Laura go to Limmeridge House, followed by Walter, who learns that Mr Fairlie has died; and Walter's son is 'the Heir of Limmeridge'.

The conventional happy ending, but not achieved without great complexity. It is only fitting that the last words should recognize the pre-eminence of Marian in the story.

## Revision questions on the Third Epoch

**1** Give an account of Marian's actions during this sequence and say what they reveal of her character.
**2** Write a fairly detailed appraisal of Walter's actions. How

far do you think he alone is responsible for bringing about the conclusion to the novel?

**3** 'Fosco ought to have been allowed to get away.' How far do you agree with the statement?

**4** Compare and contrast Mrs Catherick and Mrs Clements.

**5** Which do you consider the most dramatic incident in the Third Epoch, and why?

**6** Write an essay on Collins's ability to vary his narrative style in this epoch.

# The characters

## Walter Hartright

Let Walter Hartright, teacher of drawing, aged twenty-eight years, be heard first.

Walter is the hero of the story; he is sensitive, upright, romantic, showing great strength of mind and perseverance. He saves Pesca's life; finds his mother a more sympathetic and essentially youthful character than his sister; is a vivid writer; appears, initially, to be very taken with Marian. In fact, as the plot unfolds, we share his admiration for Marian and her spirit: we rather wonder why Walter has not fallen in love with her. He confides in her, relies on her, acts by her code of honour and accepts her standards. Because he is a teacher of drawing at Limmeridge House, he has to accept a subservient position, but he behaves with dignity and consideration at all times. He is no hypocrite, and sees through Mr Fairlie at once. His realization of his love for Laura is moving if romantic, and we experience his mixture of delight and anguish when he realizes that she loves him in return.

Walter disappears from the narrative for long periods, and is very downcast and sorry for himself when seen in London just before he commits himself to sailing for Honduras. But he has previously shown himself to be of a naturally grateful nature, appreciating not only Marian but also what Pesca has done for him in recommending him for the post at Limmeridge House. His compassion and sincerity are shown in his initial encounter with the woman in white: he readily gives her assistance and is dubious of those who are pursuing her; in fact it can be said that he humours her without any trace of condescension. Even after this he is stricken with conscience (a further underlining of his sensitivity), but his susceptibility to female charm – and the woman in white's unusual quality of being facially ugly – stands him in good stead when he later meets Marian. He displays a rare irony when contemplating Laura's former governess ('Mrs Vesey sat through life'), but all is turned to romantic wonderment when he first sees Laura ('How can I separate her from my own sensations and from all that has happend in the later time?'). But there are times when Walter is somewhat sententious, or perhaps it is that his creator is too self-consciously indulging the utterances of supposed wisdom, as in 'The grandest mountain prospect that the eye can range over is appointed to annihilation. The smallest human interest that the pure heart can feel is appointed to immortality.'

Walter compensates by being singularly sentimental over the evenings spent in the drawing-room while Laura plays Mozart. But all the while he is absorbed in the mystery of 'the woman in white', though as Laura changes emotionally towards him (because of her recognition of her own feelings), he senses in her eyes 'the prescient sadness of a coming and long farewell'. Naturally his first feeling on learning of her prior engagement to Sir Percival Glyde is one of jealousy, and he seizes on the evidence of Anne Catherick's letter that Sir Percival is someone not to be trusted.

Anne herself (the woman in white), when she meets Walter again, testifies to his kindness; despite his own love for Laura he spends much time talking sympathetically to Anne and trying to find out why she 'loses herself' at the mention of Sir Percival Glyde. Somehow it brings out a sense of his own limitations ('I had done with my poor man's touchy pride – I had done with all my little artist vanities'), though he indulges his self-pity over the short time he has left at Limmeridge House.

Walter continues to be fascinated and active in the hunt to

find out more about the mystery woman. He endures the last moving, poignant evening at Limmeridge House and, finally, the breakfast good-bye from Laura and Marian. Mr Gilmore sees Walter walking to Holborn, but it is a Walter bowed down by grief for his lost love ('His face looked pale and haggard ... his manner was hurried and uncertain ... his dress ... was so slovenly now that I should have been ashamed of the appearance of it on one of my own clerks').

Thereafter Walter disappears, missing the eventful machinations of Sir Percival and Count Fosco, and thus having to piece them together when he returns in the autumn of 1850 from the dangerous expedition to South America. He soon heads for Limmeridge House: he visits 'Laura's' grave and, in one of the masterly climaxes of the novel, sees the living Laura herself standing beside it. The result is that he succeeds in getting Laura and Marian to London and thereafter begins his determined quest to unravel the mystery.

Walter has perseverance and stamina, ingenuity and courage, is not afraid of a physical encounter, and has a true hero's capacity to endure and still triumph. He is a good story-teller, providing us with sustained narrative fluency and, of course, moments and incidents of almost unbearable suspense. He has the good sense to realize that Laura must be concealed at all costs; he shows ingenuity in enlisting the aid of Pesca when he is most needed in the attempt to reduce the Count. But Walter lacks – who can wonder at it in view of the seriousness of the matters he is involved with – a sense of humour. He is dedicated, earnest, single-minded, a good surrogate brother to Marian and the active hero-husband to his suffering wife.

## Marian Halcombe

The easy elegance of every movement of her limbs and body as soon as she began to advance ... The lady is dark ... The lady is young ... The lady is ugly!

This is how Walter sees Marian, with the 'masculine look of her features'. It is this unusual duality that makes Marian a wholly sympathetic character, who possesses none of the cloying sentimentality of her half-sister Laura Fairlie. Marian is intensely protective and loving to Laura, and becomes a real sister to Walter – while Fosco expresses undisguised admiration for Marian's charms, her integrity and her intelligence.

*The Woman in White* belongs to the year 1860 and, though Wilkie Collins is nothing if not sexually aware, it would be unwise for us to attach any label (like Lesbian, for instance) to Marian. She exists in her own right as an independent, warm, sensitive, suffering creature, remarkably fluent and able by sheer will-power to conceal her inner tumults – and we know from her diary that these are many. From her first meeting with Walter, through his initially unhappy love for Laura, she is his guide and friend, and a protectress to them both.

*The Woman in White* has been called a novel with two heroines, but of the two Marian is noticeably the more positive and consequently the more convincing; consider the clarity with which she puts Walter in the picture about the Limmeridge House situation. In return she receives his confidence about Laura, also about the woman in white, and it is largely Marian who initiates the local investigation. As a prelude to this she reads the letter to Walter that establishes the extraordinary likeness between Laura and Anne Catherick. Marian immediately recognizes Walter's love for Laura, and tells him that he must therefore leave Limmeridge House – later explaining gently, that Laura is already engaged. As we have seen, Marian is, like Walter, fascinated by the mystery of the woman in white, and she is so moved by Walter's account of his second meeting with Anne Catherick that she begins to doubt Laura's future happiness with Sir Percival Glyde.

In fact Marian becomes progressively more depressed as Laura's marriage day approaches, and her own narrative, which follows Gilmore's, is riddled with the uncertainty and fear she experiences. She comforts Laura on a number of occasions, and is the recipient by letter of Walter's misery after he has left; she also notes his determination to go to Honduras. Nevertheless, Marian is sensible enough to try to restrain Laura's love for Walter though she also seeks to stop the marriage to Sir Percival. But 'My forebodings are realised. The marriage is fixed for the 22nd December', this subsequently leads to a Woman's-lib outburst one hundred years before the burning of bras became a famous issue: 'No man under heaven deserves the sacrifices from us women. Men! They are the enemies of our innocence and our peace – they drag us away from our parents' love and our sisters' friendship – they take us body and soul to themselves, and fasten our helpless lives to theirs as they chain up a dog in his kennel.' Strong stuff for 1860, but Marian is only human, and breaks down in accepted womanly fashion afterwards. She has some compensation by finding out about Miss Eleanor Fairlie's marriage to Count Fosco, and of the latter's friendship with Sir Percival. She hates the latter, and evidence of her singular devotion to Laura is seen in the closing words of the First Epoch: 'They are gone! I am blind with crying – I can write no more –'

Marian is always susceptible to atmosphere, and her stay at Blackwater Park – particularly the incident with Mrs Catherick's dog – is reflected in her emotional tension as she waits for Laura. Her possessiveness over the latter is shown here too ('It is always Laura Fairlie who has been writing to me for the last six months, and never Lady Glyde'). Marian's sight-seeing rambles round Blackwater Park are shot through with her own brand of observant humour. She describes the place as being a 'wonderful architectural jumble', but she can also be scathingly critical of what it represents. The incident with the dog re-sharpens her sense of a mystery and recalls Walter Hartright to her mind – and her heart – again.

All this gives way to the changes she finds in Laura, her contemplation of the Eleanor Fairlie that was – now the Countess Fosco – her view of the repugnant Sir Percival and, above all, her appraisal of Count Fosco, who comes to dominate her consciousness. She is amazed and obsessed by the compelling personality of the man and the apparent contradictions in him. She also feels an inexplicable fear. Despite this, she is the one person who is equal to the Count in point of conversation and rational argument; he is, of course, delighted by this.

Marian now becomes an observer and narrator of the attempts of Sir Percival to get Laura's money, and of the Count's keeping him at bay – largely, we suspect, for his own ends. Marian has the initiative to write to Mr Kyrle, and knows later that the letter has been intercepted and scrutinized before being re-posted. She demonstrates her bravery and ingenuity when she manages to eavesdrop on a conversation between the Count and Sir Percival, in which the Count talks about the possibility of Laura dying (Second Epoch, Chapter 9, pp.338–56). Shortly after her exposure on the roof while listening to this conversation, Marian becomes ill; Mrs Michelson reports on the progress of that illness. Now Marian becomes part of the complex deception, her illness worsening for five days, improving by the tenth, after which she is apparently removed from Blackwater Park by the Foscos. In reality she remains at Blackwater under the care of the saturnine Mrs Rubelle. Marian next goes to Limmeridge House but suffers a relapse; following this she sets in train her efforts to trace the whereabouts of Laura, and here we see that quality of tenacity that distinguishes her. She does not accept the idea of Laura's death for one moment, and succeeds in getting her half-sister out of the asylum (see the section on 'Plot') and takes her to Limmeridge House, where Mr Fairlie characteristically refuses to recognize her. Typically, Marian devotes herself to Laura until the return of Walter gives solace and protection to them both.

With Walter's investigations absorbing the bulk of the last part of the novel, Marian virtually ceases to play a positive role. For all that, she remains one of the most interesting and fully conceived characters in the novel: a forthright woman of integrity and power. We feel, as the Count feels, a very strong admiration for her. And there is a psychological consistency in her presentation that underlines the fact that Wilkie Collins is much more than a mere sensation-writer.

## Count Fosco

he is immensely fat ... He is a most remarkable likeness, on a large scale, of the great Napoleon ... They are the most unfathomable grey eyes I ever saw, and they have at times a cold clear, beautiful, irresistible glitter in them which forces me to look at him, and yet causes me sensations, when I do look, which I would rather not feel.

The above is Marian's description of Count Fosco, who is in many ways the prototype villain for succeeding generations of crime writers, but who is so much more than an amalgam of characteristics. Fosco is larger than life and yet convincingly and tellingly of it. His wife worships him and dances attendance on him; and he commands a life beyond the grave, as we see at the end. He is magnetic and mesmeric, exacting obedience from his pets and yet treating them with hyperbolic verbal and physical tenderness. But nothing can save Fosco ultimately from the retribution of the Brotherhood.

From the first Fosco produces a powerful effect upon Marian, making his wife somewhat jealous (we suspect he delights in this kind of torture). He is a gourmet, and he is suave and superbly diplomatic when he finds that Laura and Marian are upset by the financial importunities of Sir

Percival. Above all, he is cunning: the chance remark of Sir Percival's that Laura and Anne Catherick resemble each other closely gives him the idea to initiate the plot that is to lead to the faked death of Laura and the inevitable confrontation with Walter. Of course there is money in it for the Count if he can so manipulate things that he has Sir Percival where he wants him; but we feel that the Count's real pleasure is in pitting his wits against those – always inferior – of other people. He fluctuates between the urbane, the sentimental and the incredibly cool: witness his treatment of Marian on the first two counts and, at the end of the book, his ability to sleep for exactly one hour when he is being sorely pressed by Walter.

Fosco is artistic and alert, always aware of the details of a situation and what they can lead to. He is never at a loss, always master of his plots and plans, so that even his return of Marian's letter to the postbox is achieved with suave unconcern – a kind of indolent aplomb, which, in its gross and grotesque way, is almost disarming. Gross and grotesque are two of the words we should most associate with Fosco; he is both, but always with that complete veneer of civilization and sophistication that masks, but does not hide, his capacity to exude sheer evil. Only once does he falter, and that is when he sees Pesca and the other man at the opera. Quite remarkable is his handling of Sir Percival; his ability to grasp a situation and calculate how best to turn it to advantage; his superb self-control on all occasions. We have refrained here from quoting at length about Fosco, but the interested student will discover a wealth of description of his physical and indeed cultural and intellectual predilections. He tends to dominate any scene in which he appears – and we use the word 'scene' advisedly, for Fosco is essentially a theatrical creation, a tribute to Collins's own considerable dramatic skill.

Fosco has, too, a sophisticated sense of humour; a fine sense of timing; a colourful and idiosyncratic control of language. If Collins is here satirizing foreign speech, it is also true that the Count's utterances are strongly individualistic in delivery and effect. Fosco is the master of words and the master of motive, an incredible creation who, from his first appearance, raises the imaginative tempo of the narrative.

## Sir Percival Glyde

a most prepossessing man, as far as manners and appearance were concerned. He looked rather older than I had expected, his head being bald over the forehead and his face somewhat marked and worn, but his movements were as active and his spirits as high as a young man's.

Despite the reader's identification with Walter, the Sir Percival as described by Mr Gilmore seems on the face of it to be an honourable man. But if Fosco is the stronger villain, Sir Percival is the traditional bad Baronet (as Anne tells Walter on their first meeting). Sir Percival's reaction to Laura's telling him she is in love with someone else shows the kind of man he is; her forthrightness and innocence cannot penetrate the determination and exertion of will that make this man hypocrite enough to conceal his real character and motives until after the marriage has taken place.

Laura is married, and Sir Percival carries her off to Italy on their honeymoon. Shortly after their return he sets in motion his plans for relieving her of the £20,000 he needs. He is rash, ill-tempered, possessive, jealous, has unpredictable moods and is several times on the edge of violence – a stereotype of villainous behaviour. The element of realism Collins occasionally lacks is nowhere more in evidence than in his presentation of the relationship between Sir Percival and Laura: we find it difficult to accept the domestic, sexual or even social reality of their existence. But since neither of them lives on the same imaginative level as Marian or Fosco, we need not, perhaps, in their case consider psychological truth too closely.

Sir Percival is short-tempered and irascible, bent on concealment of the Secret, and consequently intent on taking precautions to avoid its discovery. In effect his role is a somewhat melodramatic one, since he exists after the return from honeymoon largely as a foil to Fosco. He is of course a forger, and it is on his written addition to the marriage register that the whole plot, or rather, the necessity for it, hangs. Sir Percival is not Sir Pervical, but he has to spend the rest of his life covering that living lie; the result is that he has no security of tenure of anything – of Blackwater Park, of Laura, of Laura's money, mainly because of the tenacious presence of the Secret, which necessitates the putting away of Anne Catherick, and the purchase of her mother's silence too in return for inverted respectability. Sir Percival has to keep on the right side of Fosco as well, thus risking merely becoming the latter's dupe. He meets the end he deserves, like the evil villain of Victorian melodrama that he is.

## Laura Fairlie

A fair, delicate girl, in a pretty light dress, trifling with the leaves of a sketch-book, while she looks up from it with truthful, innocent blue eyes – that is all the drawing can say...

In a sense, Laura is a drawing: the main heroine but much less vivid than Marian; much more simply acceptable in her attraction and innocence. Laura is idealized by Walter, suffers through her love for him which comes after she has become engaged to Sir Percival, and when she seeks to remove herself from that engagement by a forthright confession that she loves another, finds that she is unable to do so because of the fixed determination cleverly masked, of the man to whom she is committed. Thus Laura gives herself up to a marriage in which she is to be violently used and abused. Sir Percival is soon made jealous of Walter; at Blackwater Park she is imprisoned in an asylum and only escapes through the courage and stong-mindedness of Marian. She survives this, but goes into a decline and is protected by Walter, whom she finally marries after the death of the wicked Sir Percival.

Laura is indeed the conventional heroine, though occasionally she shows more spirit than we would be inclined to give her credit for. She never displays a sense of humour; she is somewhat cloyingly devoted to Marian; rather indulges her feelings of abject misery over the renunciation of Walter; she is generally unacceptable as real flesh and blood. Although we sympathize with Laura's situation, it is difficult to sympathize with her as an individual, since we see her as a type rather than a person. She exists, as she does in Walter's sentimental memory, as a 'drawing', an outline rather than a fully formed woman.

## Mr Fairlie

he had a frail, languidly-fretful, over-refind look − something singularly and unpleasantly delicate in its association with a man, and, at the same time, something which could by no possibility have looked natural and appropriate if it had been transferred to the personal appearance of a woman.

Frederick Fairlie is the recluse-cum-cultural dilettante par excellence − his 'life' is really a sophisticated nullity of existence. His chief affectation is his fear of noise, and he, like Fosco but without the latter's magnetism, is one of the genuine eccentrics of *The Woman in White*. He is indolent and artistic, withdrawn from the world and consequently from human experience. The result is a devastatingly satirical and cynical portrait of a parasite. Collins does not ease up, and the tone is sustained throughout those portions of the narrative in which Mr Fairlie appears or, rather, languishes. He talks of 'pecuniary arrangements' to Walter, and speaks further of the 'entries of my tablettes', even saying, 'Gently with the curtains, please – the slightest noise from them goes through me like a knife'.

Mr Fairlie actually 'undertakes' (his word) part of the narrative, but since this involves his encounter with Fosco he is none too pleased at having to do so, prefacing his account typically with, 'It is the grand misfortune of my life that nobody will let me alone.' He has quite an ironic and satiric edge in his account of people; initially it is tinged with snobbery ('People in the lower class of life never know when or how to go out of a room.') He is suspicious of Fosco ('He looked like a walking-West-Indian-epidemic') and is relieved though exhausted when Fosco eventually takes himself off. Later, absorbed in himself and his retreat into silence, he refuses to accept the fact that Laura is still alive despite the evidence of her presence; nothing becomes him like his dying, though we wonder that he has the energy to do even that.

## Minor characters

As always with Collins, a stroke of the pen is enough to bring a character alive, and as we have seen in the section on 'Narrative art and structure', he is adept at making the style fit the man (or woman). Fosco's Postscript by a sincere friend following Marian's collapse, could only have been written by him – the style is the flamboyance of the man – while Mr Fairlie's style reflects the crochety and hypersensitive reactions which he displays to anything which threatens to encroach upon his privacy. The housekeeper *Mrs Michelson* is every whit her clergyman-husband's widow, referring to the Bible from time to time and evincing an unswerving Christian attitude towards the strange goings-on which surround her.

Duped by being sent to Torquay, she returns to give in her notice.

All Collins's characters have their particular functions within the plot and the narration, and *Madame Fosco* is no exception. She is the living demonstration of her husband's power, for she is reduced to being his slave – apart from sudden manifestations of jealousy when he shows interest in any other woman. Yet, incredibly, she comes alive by enjoying her position. She is more than useful to the Count, follows Marian, guards Laura, plays an essential part in the plot to incarcerate the latter and thus establish the false identity as *fact* – from which she and her husband and Sir Percival can derive so much benefit.

When the Count is finally tracked down and confronted by Walter, Madame Fosco asserts the superiority of her husband, whom she regards with something approaching idolatry, when he is alive and even after his death. She is the living tribute to the magnetic force of his personality and the effortless effect of his character, and in this way she is a reflection of his evil.

If Madame Fosco is a reflection of evil, *Mrs Catherick* is evil personified. In some ways she forms an admirable contrast with both Sir Percival and Mr Fairlie, for she too represents a selfishness that is unswervingly dedicated to achieving a particular way of life. The plot reveals that she formerly had an affair with the handsome Philip Fairlie; conceived a child by him; married Mr Catherick dishonestly in order to give that child a name; received the gifts that she coveted from Sir Percival; then spent a lifetime devoting herself to attaining a respectable position in her neighbourhood. Ultimately, we suppose, by this she exorcises her sin, and becomes an outward model of conventional Christian behaviour. Her bid for respectability is not dissimilar from that made in the later part of her interesting career by Becky Sharp in *Vanity Fair*, but she lacks Becky's charm, fascination, self-humour, honesty and, above all, the living bitchery that exults in what it gets from life.

Mrs Catherick is a hypocrite, her heart corroded by the effects of public scandal and the fact is that in essentials she has not been misjudged but indeed correctly interpreted by her neighbours. They merely misplaced the time of her adultery and were mistaken about her lover. All her scarcely suppressed bitterness comes out; her interview with Walter, and the letter she writes him, are both degraded by vindictive and treacherous assertions and duplicity.

Mrs Catherick's daughter *Anne* is at the centre of the web, the mysterious woman in white devoted to the memory of Mrs Fairlie who had been so kind to her (ironically, kind to her husband's child). Her strong resemblance to Laura brings her within the orbit of Count Fosco and ultimately leads to her death. The 'white' unquestionably symbolizes her innocence, her freedom from the taint of deception, though the plotters have tried to stigmatize her as tainted by arranging for her to be kept in a private asylum. Anne's mind wanders, she is liable to loss of concentration and of course bitterness when she thinks of Sir Percival. She is central throughout to the unravelling of the plot, for without her existence the Secret and the wholesale ramifications of deception that permeate the novel are as nothing. Collins conveys perfectly Anne's essential simplicity, her lack of positive volition and her innocence; the fact that none of these cloys is a tribute to his ability to fashion character from someone not fully developed, not fully integrated into life.

*Mrs Vesey*, as we have noted, sits through life in friendly interaction with her charges.

*Mrs Rubelle* is a Gothic-type character, with all the necessary turnings of mystery and threat needed for emphasis in the melodramatic area of the plot. She is not, of course, treated in any depth.

*Professor Pesca* is a delight, essential to the plot in two ways. Firstly, he is instrumental in getting Walter the job at Limmeridge House, and secondly he uncovers the story of the Brotherhood and, incidentally, the Secret of Fosco (note again the duplication of situation that characterizes Collins's narrative art). His excitable volubility, his superbly vivid coinages of mixed English/Italian, his generous nature, his simple but exuberant manner, all these make him too a genuine eccentric, in direct contrast to the mannered and urbane Fosco who conceals his guilty past.

The solicitors *Merriman, Gilmore* and *Kyrle* are interestingly presented, again in terms of contrast. Merriman represents Sir Percival and, like him, is intent on getting his own way, not minding what unscrupulous methods he has to employ to achieve his ends. Gilmore is a serious and wise man, seeing into the heart of the Glyde matter, but nevertheless acting with caution and in a rational and balanced way. There is nothing more moving in this novel than his recognition of Laura's suffering. His heart goes out to her, as ours to him, at the thought of her devoting her life misguidedly to Sir Percival – and in addition being financially coerced. Kyrle is the recipient of Marian's letter, and gives here much sound advice, though he later forthrightly points out to Walter how difficult it would be in fact to prove that Laura is alive.

All the minor characters contribute basically to the *atmosphere* of the novel and, as we have said, each has a function in the somewhat tortuous unravellings of the plot and in the overall narrative structure of the novel.

# Structure and style

## Structure

In terms of English fiction Wilkie Collins is something of an innovator of narrative form, although there are a number of 18th-century novels in which more than one narrator is employed. Samuel Richardson (1689–1761), author of *Pamela* and *Clarissa*, used the epistolary form, which requires more than one letter-writer to tell the story, since letters once written have to be replied to even in the world of fiction. In one sense this is an anticipation of Collins's own literary art in *The Woman in White* (notice indeed the significance of the letters here in terms of plot revelation). Seven years before its publication Collins's great friend Charles Dickens had employed a dual narrative mode in *Bleak House*, where the omniscient author relates one part of the story while Esther Summerson, the rather vapid heroine, writes the other; in fact, in chapter totals alone, they share the narrative.

Collins extends and refines this concept, so that many voices speak to us, from the central figures (Walter Hartright and Marian Halcombe) to transient characters who are there to verify facts and make statements (the doctor and the cook). Significantly, it is fundamentally the good characters who have the most say, that is, those with a central moral orientation. Since they command the bulk of the narration they direct and condition the reader's responses to events and revelations. The evil characters – Fosco, Sir Percival, Mrs Catherick – have little or no say, except that Fosco writes briefly Marian's diary and later produces an account of his activities for Walter. The first is a verbal self-indulgence of his feelings for Marian, the second a necessary linking to bring the reader up to date on exactly what has occurred. Mrs Catherick's letter is a confirmation of some of her own wickedness and hypocrisy.

The choice of narrators is very much a part of Collins's method; we cannot, for example, imagine Sir Percival writing an account, nor could we endure one from Laura. Walter Hartright tells the story on pp.34–150; Mr Gilmore the solicitor, pp.150–84; Marian from p.184 via her diary to the end of the First Epoch on p.217, then into the Second Epoch, pp. 219–358. Then Fosco's postscript on 21 June follows for a couple of pages; this takes us to a high point of tension, after which Frederick Fairlie takes up the tale in his effeminate and whimsical manner, thus adding considerably to the humour of the narrative – a kind of equivalent to the porter's scene in *Macbeth*, a delaying tactic before we come to the real discoveries.

This somewhat lighter tone continues, pp.360–78, its linking function reinforced by Mrs Michelson whose account follows on pp.379 to 420, with cook, doctor, Jane Gould and the inscription on the tombstone giving us all the facts before Walter resumes the narrative on p.426. The Second Epoch closes on p.431 with the most dramatic moment in the novel: Walter's meeting with Laura beside what purports to be her gravestone.

The Third and final Epoch opens on the following page and effectively continues through to the end, though inevitably it includes what Walter has learned from Marian, while Mrs Catherick contributes her own story in the form of a letter to Walter that occupies some twelve pages. Fosco's papers, too, are put into Walter's hands, and again the retrospective account supplies all the details of Fosco's motives and the initiation of the plot to get rid of Laura, even down to the detail of the near mishap because of the error in timing. From then on Walter takes over and thus has the bulk of the narrative.

This method is aesthetically and dramatically satisfying on a number of counts. Firstly, it enables the story to be treated flexibly from the chronological point of view by providing retrospective narration at the appropriate moment and giving the reader the clues which may have been missed or lost in the previous narrative. Secondly, it allows a nice blend of the factual and the imaginative, a balancing of the commonplace and the dramatic. Thirdly, it provides an insight into character and motive as each narrator takes up the particular thread of his own concerns. Above all, the method gives a kind of perspective impossible in a narrative that is limited to the perceptions of a single character, recording situations seen from one viewpoint only.

So the advantages and the variety of Collins's method are apparent: romance, change of mood, revelation, subjective analysis reinforced or contradicted by later revelation or discovery – all these are possible and *complementary* in a many-sided narrative. There is an increase in tension, for example, for dramatic tension is engendered by a number of elements, perhaps the chief of which is surprise.

Walter's encounters with Anne Catherick; with Laura at her own grave; with Fosco in the house in St John's Wood; his arrival at the fire that destroys Sir Percival: all these are the experiences of one narrator, and each has the dramatic element of crisis on which the successful sensation novel depends.

These crises are complemented in the narratives of Marian; seriously in that of Gilmore; lightly in that of Mr Fairlie; retrospectively in those of Mrs Catherick and Fosco.

There is a certain unity in the story that enables Collins to expolit to the full the elements of coincidence and duplication which contribute to the structural coherence of the book. Walter saves Pesca, Fosco saves Sir Percival, and the contrasting effects of these rescues are seen as their dramas unfold.

The saving of Pesca leads ultimately to the exposure of Fosco; good triumphs over evil, in accordance with the convention of the period.

The structure further includes two heroines and two villains: the memory of Mrs Fairlie provides poignant contrast in goodness with the vituperative and living Mrs Catherick; while Frederick Fairlie, hypochondriac and collector extraordinary, may be contrasted with Baldassare Fosco, gourmet and collector of pets and arias – the novel is rich in these echoing associations, Wilkie Collins, acknowledging his Gothic predecessors, deliberately cultivates the sensational and macabre affiliations of death: witness the tending of Mrs Fairlie's grave by Anne; her meeting in the churchyard with Walter; Walter's later meeting with Laura by the gravestone; the contemplation, which the reader shares, of Fosco in the morgue.

This use of the sensational goes hand-in-hand with that of the romantic, while the sentimental and the determinedly eccentric also exist together. The introduction of the Brotherhood provides further evidence of the depths at which the author worked, for this is yet another area of duplication: retribution and justice on the wider political front, as distinct from the personal and moral level; Fosco rightly being the victim of the first as Sir Percival Glyde is of the second.

Consider, too, the structure seen in terms of the physical (certainly evident in the contrasting characters) but also in the central focus on the two houses of Limmeridge and Blackwater Park – even their names reflect the different moralities of their inhabitants. The student should examine Walter's account of Limmeridge House and Marian's often satirical description of Blackwater Park to taste the real flavour of the contrast.

The overall effect is that of a highly organized novel in which action, situation and revelation are brought into coherence within the building of narrative tension. The different voices each have something new to add to the plot, to further the mystery or the menace, linking past and present until every strand of the narrative is tied in. Collins's sense of form is a sophisticated one and, because of his method, he has no need to adopt the role (of the all-seeing, all-powerful author) played by his contemporary novelists. His voice and his concerns are felt through his narrators, so the moral import of the novel – that the action is basically a contest between good and evil, and that good must win – is never forgotten.

*The Woman in White* is not merely experimental; strangely, it anticipates much of our 20th-century fiction. The 'stream of consciousness' here flows through a number of narrative channels just as it does in the work of James Joyce, Virginia Woolf or D. H. Lawrence. There is, of course, a tremendous technical difference, but Walter, Marian, Fosco and Fairlie each reveal themselves through their consciousness and their concerns just as surely as do Stephen and Leopold and Molly Bloom. We should remember that Wilkie Collins was writing before psychology was a cult word and before sexuality could be overtly mentioned, even in polite terms, in a novel. Today his methods may seem somewhat strained to us but we must not forget the demands of the conventions by which he wrote. His sense of form and structure, his artistic awareness, carry a certain validity, a truth perhaps for our own time, when permissiveness and ·elf-indulgent writing can reduce the artist and degrade his art.

## Style

Wilkie Collins is an unusual stylist for his time. The salient feature of his writing is its uncomplicated direct lucidity, whether he is expressing himself in description, narration, or exchanges of dialogue. Imagery, that standby of the imagina-

tive writer, is but sparsely used in *The Woman in White*, and
when it is, it is of a somewhat trite nature ('My seat was on
thorns, and my soul was on fire to speak'). Collins has a
superb control of direct narration, and this is only occasionally interrupted by rational or rhetorical flourishes that pass
for generalizations: 'We don't want genius in this country,
unless it is accompanied by respectability.' At the same time
he is a master of the unexpected, taking, we imagine, a mis-
chievous delight in encouraging the reader to arrive at the
wrong conclusion. Here is Walter Hartright's – and the
reader's – first glimpse of Marian Halcombe:

She turned towards me immediately. The easy elegance of every
movement of her limbs and body as soon as she began to advance
from the far end of the room, set me in a flutter of expectation to see
her face clearly. She left the window – and I said to myself, The lady
is dark. She moved forward a few steps – and I said to myself, The
lady is young. She approached nearer – and I said to myself (with a
sense of surprise which words fail me to express), The lady is ugly!
(p.58)

But Collins's general method is far removed from this. He is
direct and exact, conveying the *facts* of an action or reaction in
brief compass, though often with some recourse to a kind of
moral commentary: 'I sat down at once to write the letter,
expressing myself in it as civilly, as clearly, and as briefly as
possible. Mr Fairlie did not hurry his reply. Nearly an hour
elapsed before the answer was placed in my hands' (p.133).
The telling phrase here is 'as civilly, as clearly, and as briefly
as possible', because it defines Collins's mode of narrative, in
an age of novels that were for the most part wordy and
cumbersome – 'loose, baggy monsters', as Henry James described the lengthy Victorian novel.

Collins was just as succinct when it came to the use of
dialogue; inevitably, with the passage of time, some exchanges
now seem mannered, but there is evidence that his own

interest in writing plays gave him a natural ear when it came to recording the varieties of human intonation. This facility enabled him to make his character distinctions clear. Characters as diverse as Count Fosco, Sir Percival Glyde, Mr Merriman or, most distinctively, Mr Fairlie, could by no means be mistaken one for the other.

Consideration of Mr Fairlie brings us happily to an aspect of Collins's style that is unprepossessing but impressive: the delicacy of his irony when he is dealing with that frailest of mortals, whose mind is as supine as his collection is arid. If the Count is the frightening eccentric par excellence, with menace in every nuance of his suave fluency, then Fairlie's words are languid with his own anti-life withdrawal. In Collins the spoken word reveals the character, each narrator is given an individual stamp of identity through his utterance.

Collins, the son of an artist father, is a painter in words, though more through description than imagery. His evocation of atmosphere — sometimes Gothic, full of foreboding, sometimes as the natural counterpoint to the mood or situation of a character — is magnificent. Here is Walter somewhere near the heart of the mystery:

The clouds were wild in the western heaven, and the wind blew chill from the sea. Far as the shore was, the sound of the surf swept over the intervening moorland, and beat drearily in my ears as I entered the churchyard. Not a living creature was in sight. The place looked lonelier than ever when I chose my position, and waited and watched, with my eyes on the white cross that rose over Mrs Fairlie's grave. (p.116)

Collins also uses retrospect to fill in the gaps of the narrative, also to lay his clues more fully before the reader, as with Mrs Clements's account of her journey with Anne, or Walter's picking up the narrative of his sheltering Laura and Marian in London. In fact Collins's style is remarkable for its variety:

dialect in Cumberland ('T' ghaist of Mistress Fairlie'); the romantic mood as befits a young man in love ('the touch of the golden autumn wound its bright way visibly through the green summer of the trees'); the diary style of Marian Halcombe (almost a continuation of Richardson's narrative epistolary mode, say in *Pamela* or *Clarissa*), or the simple factuality of Hester Pinhorn, cook.

As an example of the variety of Collins's narrative art, note the rhetorical flourish, a kind of literary crescendo, with which he treats that prototype of all villains, Count Fosco:

There he lay, unowned, unknown, exposed to the flippant curiosity of the French mob! There was the dreadful end of that long life of degraded ability and heartless crime! Hushed in the sublime repose of death, the broad, firm, massive face and head fronted us so grandly that the chattering Frenchwomen about me lifted their hands in admiration, and cried in shrill chorus, 'Ah, what a handsome man!' The wound that had killed him had been struck with a knife or a dagger exactly over his heart. No other traces of violence appeared about the body except on the left arm, and there, exactly in the place where I had seen the brand on Pesca's arm, were two deep cuts in the shape of the letter T, which entirely obliterated the mark of the Brotherhood. His clothes, hung above him, showed that he had been himself conscious of his danger – they were clothes that had disguised him as a French artisan. For a few moments, but not for longer, I forced myself to see these things through the glass screen. I can write of them at no greater length, for I saw no more. (p.643)

We have chosen this passage because it provides the opportunity for a close texual study of Collins; moreover it both sums up and epitomizes Collins's main stylistic skills. Here we are not in the world of Moriarty or Carl Petersen, for though both Sherlock Holmes and Bulldog Drummond respect and admire their adversaries despite their villainy, they do not love them. But at this moment there is a feeling akin to unphysical love in Hartright for his enemy – a feeling engendered by Collins.

There is a unique combination here of simplicity and sublimity, of the intrigue of the Brotherhood and the self-honesty of the writer ('I can write of them at no greater length...') There is, too, a splendid command of pathos; paradoxically we feel the loss of Fosco's larger-than-life, gentler-than-life cruelty, his attentions to his pets, his dominance of his wife, his admiration of Marian. With all the physical disadvantages of his immense size (and of age) he has still *compelled* us, just as he has compelled those with whom he has come into contact. Even after his death his fascination continues – and the Frenchwomen in the crowd at the Morgue (a year after Madame Defarge and her guillotine Furies were set before the reading public in *A Tale of Two Cities*), exclaim, 'Ah, what a handsome man!', as we see above.

This passage represents Collins at his very best, where fact and direct description ('The wound that had killed him') are mingled with a sense of awe at the sight of the dead man who in life had been so potent. Collins has been accused of using too many words at times, but his descriptive style has a fine economy.

# General questions and sample answer in note form

**1** Compare and contrast Marian and Laura.

**2** Which of the narrators in *The Woman in White* do you find most interesting and why? In your answer refer closely to the text.

**3** Write a detailed character analysis of Count Fosco and the part he plays in the plot of the novel.

**4** In your opinion, what characteristics make Walter Hartright an attractive or an unattractive hero?

**5** Summarize the plot of *The Woman in White* indicating which parts of it you find most fascinating and why.

**6** In what ways do you think the title of the novel is the right one? What other choices might have been made?

**7** Write an essay on Collins's skill in creating atmosphere in *The Woman in White*.

**8** In what ways is the novel humorous? In your answer refer closely to the text.

**9** Compare and contrast Mr Fairlie and Sir Percival Glyde.

**10** Compare and contrast Mrs Catherick and Madame Fosco.

**11** In what ways is *surprise* the most important element in *The Woman in White*?

**12** Consider the parts played by the solicitors in *The Woman in White*.

**13** 'The weakness of *The Woman in White* is the woman herself.' Discuss.

**14** Explain how Wilkie Collins maintains dramatic tension in this book.

**15** Write an essay on Collins's use of the eccentric or the grotesque in *The Woman in White*.

**16** Compare and contrast Blackwater Park and Limmeridge House.

**17** Write an appreciation of Collins's narrative art in this novel.

**18** 'Too long-winded.' With regard to *The Woman in White*, defend Collins from this accusation.

**19** In what way does Collins employ dramatic devices in this novel?

**20** Write an essay on Collins's use of dialogue in *The Woman in White*.

*Suggested notes for essay answer to question 1*

**(a)** *Introduction* – say how we as readers first come to meet them – define their relationship – give Walter's description of each – Marian and her personality – Laura and hers.

**(b)** *Need of each for the other* – compare/contrast their social personalities – Marian much the stronger – more outgoing – sympathy – generosity – ability to think and evaluate – reserves of strength – feeling for Walter – resistance to Sir Percival – capable of independent thought, courage, etc.

**(c)** *Laura* – more withdrawn – shy – weighed down by burden of coming marriage to Sir Percival – love for Marian – eventual admission of love for Walter – not so strong as Marian – but individual actions show she is not without reserves of strength. Reaction to Sir Percival – telling him of her love for Walter.

**(d)** *Marian and her narrative* – pivot of action – strong-minded and practical – continuing courage – sees into Fosco. Then Laura after her marriage – meeting with Anne – looking after Marian – ill herself, etc.

*Conclusion* – use quotes to bring out differences but emphasize strength of bond between them – Marian pre-eminent in last sequences – Laura weaker (though still ill) – Marian's fortitude and her assumption of power (actually saves Laura from asylum), etc.

# Further reading

*The Moonstone*, Wilkie Collins (Penguin)
*Wilkie Collins, The Critical Heritage*, ed. by Norman Page (Routledge & Kegan Paul, 1974).
*Wilkie Collins*, Kenneth Robinson (Davis-Poynter, 1951, reprinted 1974).
*The Secret Life of Wilkie Collins*, William Clarke (Allison & Busby, 1988).